HER MAJESTY THE QUEEN
The Story of Elizabeth II

HER MAJESTY
THE QUEEN
The Story of Elizabeth II

By HELEN CATHCART

ILLUSTRATED WITH PHOTOGRAPHS

DODD, MEAD & COMPANY
NEW YORK
1962

CONTENTS

ILLUSTRATIONS

HER MAJESTY THE QUEEN

The Story of Elizabeth II

THE BABY OF BRUTON STREET

IN THE EARLY SPRING of the year 1926 George V sat upon the throne of England. Only his daughter, Princess Mary, the present Princess Royal, had so far given him grandsons and only one of his four surviving sons was married. Yet for seventy years the male succession had seldom seemed more secure.

In his thirty-second year, the Prince of Wales had just returned from an energetic tour of Africa and South America, completing his education, as he remarked, on the trade routes of the world. Aged thirty, the Duke of York busily visited the bleak industrial areas of Britain, inspected factories, organized democratic youth camps and had earned a popular title as "the Industrial Prince." In their middle twenties, King George's younger sons, Prince Henry (who became the Duke of Gloucester) and handsome Prince George (the former Duke of Kent) successfully followed their respective careers in the Services.

Flat-topped buses and cars square as packing crates

poured out to Richmond Park, where fair-weather sight-seers always waited in the hope of getting a glimpse of the Duke and Duchess of York outside White Lodge, their first married home. The passage of three years since the splendour of their Westminster Abbey wedding, and an absence of five months in East Africa, had in no way lessened public interest in the married pair. The mere whisper that the little Duchess might be anticipating a baby brought inquisitive groups who stood expectantly on every commanding knoll, unaware that their quarry had fled.

Though the Duke of York stood second to the Crown —the young couple ironically had no convenient home of their own. Living out of suitcases, at Glamis, at Balmoral, at St. Paul's Walden Bury, and Sandringham, with a staff who unpacked and repacked, they stayed for a time with Princess Mary in Chesterfield House and then settled in Curzon House, Curzon Street. "It would be very nice," the Duchess supposedly said, "if we could live in the Queen's Dolls' House."

When the happiness of a future baby became assured, the Duke hastily rented No. 40 Grosvenor Square from a Mrs. Hoffmann. There was thus a real prospect that the future Queen Elizabeth might have been born in what is now the heart of London's little America, but the Duchess of York finally decided that she wished her baby to be born in her parents' London home at 17 Bruton Street.

Queen Mary and King George approved this arrangement. Mayfair in 1926 was still essentially a region of private residences, exclusive and even aristocratic. The names of the Earl and Countess of Sandwich, Viscountess (Evelyn) de Vesci, Lady Lucas, the Herberts, the Stonors, Tennants and Pakenhams and Windhams glimmered on

polished brass plates or were listed discreetly in Boyle's
Court Guide. Carriages with ducal crests still mingled with
the boxlike limousines that turned into Bond Street and
Berkeley Square. And on the southern side of the street
the residence of the fourteenth Earl of Strathmore and
Kinghorne stood out fittingly among the dignified brick
Georgian houses, a mansion both double-fronted and stone-
faced with a line of Grecian columns across the façade proclaiming its ancestral opulence and family tradition.

The Duke and Duchess took up residence at No. 17 after
spending January at Sandringham. Any formal announcement of their hopes would have been unseemly. An irrelevant news item simply mentioned in December that,
owing to the death of Queen Alexandra, the Duchess of
York had cancelled her visit to view the new frieze by Ger-
ald Moira, in the main entrance hall of the Army and
Navy Stores. The public were left to make what they could
of the Duchess's withdrawal from public life, although the
bush telegraph of Society functioned efficiently. The fact
that the Duke and Duchess lunched with the King and
Queen on April 19th was of pointed news interest; and
in mid-April the illustrated magazines regaled their readers with photographic spreads of the Yorks without ex-
planation.

The birth of the little Princess Elizabeth has been
poetically described as "occurring in spring, at its brightest
and gayest." In sober truth, Arnold Bennett recorded,
"The weather has been evil for a week." The pavements
were still wet when the obstetric surgeons gathered at Bruton Street: Sir Henry Simson, surgeon to the Hospital for
Women; Sir George Blacker, obstetric physician to University College Hospital, and Mr. Walter Jagger, of the

Samaritan Hospital for Women. They consulted together and "a certain line of treatment"—probably a Caesarean section—"was successfully adopted."

After the confinement, the Home Secretary, Sir William Joynson-Hicks, who was present in the house, issued the first public statement to herald our present Queen: "Her Royal Highness The Duchess of York was safely delivered of a Princess at 2.40 A.M. this morning, Wednesday, April 21st." At Windsor Castle, the duty equerry, Captain Reginald Seymour, obeyed instructions and awakened the King and Queen at 4 A.M. to tell them the news. "Such a relief and joy," wrote Queen Mary.

The Lord Mayor of London was the first to be officially informed of the new Princess, and at the Tower and in Hyde Park a twenty-one-gun salute was fired to honour the King's first granddaughter. At Bruton Street, that morning, Princess Mary was the baby's first visitor outside the household. The King and Queen motored up from Windsor that afternoon and were delighted with the infant . . . "a little darling with a lovely complexion and fair hair." Intent on the occupant of the cot, the royal grandmother may not have noticed the plebeian view from the top-floor nursery, southward over the chimneys and rooftops of mews and courtyards towards Grafton Street. The nursery has vanished, the view dissolved, and now we can only measure the birthplace of Queen Elizabeth II as a vague point in space, somewhere behind the massive brickwork of Berkeley Square House, somewhere above the brick, stone, and marble facing and lush interior décor of the First National City Bank of New York, where flowers are always grouped beneath a commemorative mural in the foyer.

The possibility that the April night had seen the advent of a future Queen Regnant occurred to few. Far from ushering in an era, *The Times* devoted its editorials next day to "A Warning to Ratepayers" and "The State of Russia," while the news columns rested on the mention that the "little Princess of Great Britain and Ireland" affected the position of her younger uncles in the Succession. Two days later *The Times* reprinted the official bulletin: "The Duchess of York and the infant Princess have both had an excellent night. Their progress is in every way normal and satisfactory. Henry Simson. Walter Jagger." Although the "Mayor and Citizens" of Westminster quickly conveyed the congratulations on the birth of a Princess in the City of Westminster, the common view was that the new baby was third in succession to the Throne *for the time being,* with no prospect of improvement.

In the family, the Duchess had wanted a daughter, and the Duke of York wrote to his mother confessing their "tremendous joy. We always wanted a child to make our happiness complete, and now that it has at last happened, it seems so wonderful and strange. I am so proud of Elizabeth after all she has gone through during the last few days, and I am so thankful that everything has happened as it should and so successfully." The Queen's reply was to pay her granddaughter a second visit; and after two further assurances of "satisfactory progress," the medical bulletins were discontinued.

Two weeks later, on Saturday, May 29th, the baby Princess was christened in the private chapel at Buckingham Palace. The day was propitiously fine for the little Prin-

cess, and the sun, shining into the chapel, glinted on columns and altar cross wreathed with white and crimson
flowers. The eighteen-inch gold lily font of 1840 was
brought from Windsor and filled with ceremonial water
from the Jordan. The baby wore the christening robe of
cream Brussels lace that had been used for the children
of Queen Victoria, of Edward VII, of George V, and Princess Mary, and the ceremony was performed by the Archbishop of York. "Of course, poor baby cried," Queen
Mary noted. Informed beforehand of the names—Elizabeth Alexandra Mary—the King had noticed that Victoria
was not mentioned and "hardly thought it necessary."
Elizabeth, too, was chosen less as the mother's name than
because "it is such a nice name and there has been no one
of that name in your family for a long time," as the Duke
of York tactfully wrote, in seeking his father's consent to
it. The six sponsors were the King and Queen and Lord
Strathmore as grandparents, Princess Mary and Lady Elphinstone as aunts, and Queen Victoria's third son, the
seventy-six-year-old Duke of Connaught.

A few newspapers published photographs of the single-
tier christening cake, with its conventional cherubs and
white roses of York, and its surmounting miniature silver
cradle containing a baby doll. But public interest was now
wandering from Bruton Street, and the baby could soon be
taken for her first airing along the gravel paths of Berkeley Square, in the arms of her nurse, without attracting
attention. Immensely capable, tall and calm, putting up
with no nonsense from anyone, Mrs. Knight—known to
everyone as Alah—ruled her nursery domain with undis-
puted confidence, regardless whether her charge was third
in succession or completely remote from it. She was the

daughter of a tenant farmer on the Strathmore estate, St. Paul's Walden Bury, and she had been nanny to the Duchess of York—the present Queen Mother—to her brother, David, and to all the Elphinstone children.

After the early summer months at the Strathmore London home, Princess Elizabeth of York was first taken to Scotland, travelling up by a day train, in early August. "Big blue eyes, tiny ears and whitest skin in the world," a family friend described her at the time. At Glamis, every afternoon, she slept amid the clipped yews of the Dutch Garden, remaining with Lady Strathmore and Alah while her parents visited friends. Back in London a friend one day found the Duchess of York kneeling on the floor in front of a couch, playing with her baby, and we have this six-months-old glimpse. No doubt about it, a Princess. She was sitting up by herself in the middle of the huge chesterfield, like a white fluff of thistledown. Her hair was very fair and beginning to curl charmingly—owing, the Duchess said, to the untiring attention of her nurse. The baby was always good, she had the sweetest air of complete serenity.

Such pleasures were fleeting, for the insistent demands of royal duty now confronted the parents. The Prime Minister of Australia had asked the King if one of his elder sons would open the Parliament buildings in the new federal capital. Since the Prince of Wales had already toured Australia the opportune choice clearly fell on the Duke of York and his Duchess, and the central ceremony developed in accumulated invitations and in the immense distances of sea travel into a six-months tour. So the young mother played with her baby, saddened by the thought of all the enjoyable months of babyhood to be denied to her. The mere difficulties of communication made separation all the harder to bear. Cables could flash around the world, but sea-borne letters with photographs would take weeks. Although the two sets of doting grandparents who were to share the baby promised to mail photographs every month, the likenesses would inevitably reach the parents a month out of date. The Duchess gave her daughter a necklace of coral beads as a parting Christmas gift and it appears in the many pictures of this time like a secret code signal. "I felt very much leaving," the Duchess wrote with emotion from the ship. "The baby was so sweet playing with the buttons on Bertie's uniform that it quite broke me up."

The baby was taken to the Duchess's old familiar nursery in Hertfordshire for January and into residence at Buckingham Palace in early February. So, curiously, Elizabeth went to live in the Palace twenty-five years to the month before she first went there as Queen. The nursery lately occupied by the Harewoods was suitable for her reception and Alah carried her ward down to the Queen every day at tea-time. "Here comes the bambino!" Queen Mary would exclaim. As the weather improved, the infant was taken out every afternoon in a carriage which drove baby and nurse up Constitution Hill and down Rotten Row. In March, King George V wrote to the parents, "Your sweet little daughter . . . is growing daily. She has four teeth now, which is quite good at eleven months old, she is very happy. . . ." To which the Duke sensibly rejoined, "I do hope you will not spoil her too much, as I have always been told grandfathers are apt to."

But the spoiling came from afar, not least from the Australians and New Zealanders, who could not know they would one day be among Queen Elizabeth's Commonwealth peoples. It was a simple courtesy to mention the child in speeches of welcome, but at nearly each point of their tour the Duke and Duchess were touched by the cheers given for their little daughter, the constant inquiries after her, the shoal of letters written by children asking for photographs of "Princess Betty." Few were the ceremonies without a presentation of toys for the Princess, and no less than three tons quickly accumulated, besides carved native models, canaries, parrots, and other gifts. (The bulk were later sent to the Mayor of Durham for distribution to hundreds of needy homes.) This softened the separation, and the parents delightedly received the news of the baby's first birthday party and were told how the small Harewood boys helped to wolf the white angel cake.

In May, when the infant Princess went to stay at St. Paul's Walden Bury, the grandparents could write of her highly individual method of locomotion, not crawling but sitting on one leg and paddling vigorously with the other. In the nursery quarters beyond a green baize door, the Princess enjoyed playing a game with the two chow dogs, Brownie and Blackie, burying her fists first in the light fur of the one and then the dark fur of the other and crowing at the comparison. Alah is credited with trying desperately to teach her to say "Mother" in time for the homecoming.

When the parents returned on June 27th, 1927, little Elizabeth was awaiting them at Buckingham Palace. But the London crowds insisted on staging a more personal welcome at 145 Piccadilly, now at last ready for occupation as the future York home. A Persian carpet was hurriedly draped over the balcony, a window opened, and the "little Duchess" carried her baby out to help acknowledge the cheers of the people.

From Glamis that summer the Duchess could write to a friend, "Elizabeth is learning to walk. Very dangerous!" Alah did not believe in hurrying her charges forward. Regular nursery routine, placidity and, as soon as a child could understand, the necessity of always thinking of others were among her prime maxims. This was the period of the early Marcus Adams photographs, still enchanting after the passage of some thirty-five years. Already able to remain content and quietly observant, the little girl needed no persuasion to sit, chin cupped in chubby hand, watching the toy ducks in the studio pool.

A visitor gives us a brief sight of her, aged two, in the nursery, with its big airy windows overlooking the tree-tops: "She stood so sweetly and without the slightest shyness, waiting to be kissed." The Duchess joined in a game, each pushing a pram around the nursery table, one containing a doll, the other a teddy bear. But it did not suit little Lilibet to see her visitor left out. "Lady, too, Mummy, lady, too!" she persisted, and was not content until the guest was also duly provided with a vehicle and enlisted in this glorious fun.

An Indian writer once observed that British children live in purdah, rigidly excluded from adult life. But Lilibet's nursery—the pet name derived from the child's first lisping "Lilliebeth"—received frequent visitors, and from Glamis to Birkhall, St. Paul's Walden Bury to Naseby, where the Yorks rented a house for the hunting season, toddler and nanny followed the royal parents. When King

George V fell seriously ill with a lung infection in the winter of 1928-9 one of the tokens of his recovery was that he asked to have little Elizabeth with him, and the Princess and her nurse went to stay with the convalescent at Craigweil, near Bognor. "G. delighted to see her," the Queen wrote, fondly. Lilibet, too, was delighted to play in the garden with her grandmother, making sandpies, and the Archbishop of Canterbury thought it notable to record that he came upon them thus engaged. The King began to walk about again, one finger finding steadiness on the tiny child's arm. Her third birthday was the signal for His Majesty to resume writing his journal, and both here and in his letters references to "our sweet little grandchild" become frequent. When the convalescent monarch made his first brief appearance in public on the sea wall, a group of onlookers were delighted to see him with the Princess and "there was great cheering." Princess Elizabeth's photographs, her pictures on chocolate boxes, the magic of the printed word and the camera, and a wealth of legendary nursery lore were endearing her to the people faster than the Royal Family could believe possible. When the Duke of York had occasion to take up residence at Holyrood early that summer general disappointment that Lilibet was not also in Scotland was manifest.

"I fear that it has been a very great disappointment to the people," the Duchess wrote. "Not that they would have seen her, but they would have liked to feel that she was here. . . . It almost frightens me that the people should love her so much. I suppose that it is a good thing, and I hope she will be worthy of it, poor little darling."

If loyal Scots were dismayed at the absence of the Princess, they were to be amply compensated. Easter Monday in 1930 coincided with Lilibet's fourth birthday and a party gathering of young cousins at Windsor Castle. Outside on the terrace, the strolling crowds had the amusement of seeing the Princess respond to the salute of the Scots Guards as they marched away after the Changing of the Guard. As Queen she was later to receive the salute of many regiments, but the Scots Guards can thus claim the first honour.

Precisely four months later—on August 21st—Princess Margaret was born at Glamis. But the Duke of York had evidently cherished some hope of having a son, for the parents had not had time to agree on the names for a girl. Princess Elizabeth may have been given some hint of the prospect of a baby brother and a full day passed before she was told that she had a baby sister instead.

CHAPTER II

THE LITTLE PRINCESS

During the next seven warm and impressionable years
145 Piccadilly in London and the Royal Lodge, Windsor, became the unchanging and assured setting of Princess
Elizabeth's childhood. Number 145, by no means the
largest of the mansions that stood in the firm and substantial grandeur of Portland stone at the western end of Piccadilly, lacked the pretension of its Rothschild neighbour,
but shared a cobbled forecourt with Viscount Allendale
and others.

The Princess was more acquainted with the back door,
leading into the privacy of Hamilton Gardens and thence
into the spaces of Hyde Park, than with the brown-carpeted
entrance hallway where the two tusks of the elephant that
Papa had shot in Uganda stood on either side and wild
horses rampaged in a heavy gilt picture-frame. The innumerable adult visitors were ushered by a footman into the
morning-room on the ground floor adjoining the Duke's
study. Opening on to a circular landing on the top floor,

the convenient stabling space of a troop of toy horses, the nurseries enjoyed a sunny aloofness of their own.

Child occupants and visitors alike used the cherry carpet for seating as frequently as the chairs, although one of the smaller chairs could tinkle a tune if anyone sat in it. Here was the rocking-chair reserved for Alah and the same mahogany table and glass-fronted toy cupboard later used in the Clarence House nursery. Among the pictures Margaret Tarrant's tender study of "The Child" gazed benignly down.

From the windows the Princess could watch the largest traffic space of central London, the sinewy horses of the brewer's drays, the last of the open-topped buses, the distant ambulances pulling in to St. George's Hospital.

The Duke and Duchess of York, however, keenly felt the need of a country home for the children, and in September, 1931, when Princess Margaret was just over one year old, the King proposed the Regency pavilion of the Royal Lodge in Windsor Great Park. This was in a sad state of repair, and another year passed before the builders had added new wings and it could be occupied. But then the place became the cynosure of the life the Duchess has always intended for her children, where the long untroubled days would be remembered as an eternal summer. The reflection from the wide stone terrace filled the house with light through the tall French windows. Visiting with a photographer's eye, Lisa Sheridan noted the rocking-horses in the hall, the net curtains that "fluttered out in the gentle breeze . . . one caught on a rose-bush . . . the tap-tap of the tiny acorns on the pulleys of the blinds."

In the garden the Princess soon had a house of her own, the delightful thatch-roofed cottage, built to quarter-scale,

which was a gift from the people of Wales on her sixth
birthday. An adult could not stand upright in this miniature dwelling and the child was encouraged to keep it in
order herself, dusting, cleaning and polishing. The in-
conspicuous help from the grown-ups decreased as her
domestic skills deepened. Proudly visitors could be shown
around, provided, of course, that they stooped. "Inside
the entrance hall a diminutive grandfather clock tick-
tocked softly. The hall table held a tray for visiting-cards
and a little bowl of fresh flowers. In the delightful panelled
living-room everything was in its proper place . . . a paint-
ing of the Princesses' mother over the fireplace . . . not a
speck of dust anywhere. . . . In the bedrooms, upstairs, a
bed and a cot stood side by side, and there were brushes
and a hand-mirror on the dressing-table." So Miss Sheridan
saw the "Little House" when it was fresh and new.

Taught to take pride in this wonderful plaything, Princess Elizabeth would fling the windows open to the air
whenever she entered, as she had seen her mother do, or
drape miniature dust-covers over the furniture if she were
going away. It could be seen that she would need restraint
and forbearance when she introduced Princess Margaret
to the fragile contents of this domain, yet Alah and the
nursery staff fostered her protective, companionable, un-
selfish attitude towards her young sister until it became
second nature. "I shall call her Bud," Lilibet had confided
shortly after Princess Margaret Rose's christening. "You
see, she isn't really a rose yet. She's only a bud."

In this junior world, the under-nurse, Margaret Macdonald, had been joined by her sister, Ruby, who became
the new baby's special nursemaid. At 145 and at Windsor

this hierarchy, headed by Alah—with Smith, the nursery-maid—now formed the four corner-posts of the affectionate universe. Mrs. Knight (Alah), kindly and utterly dedicated, ruled with stern and jealous firmness. When she fell ill with flu, the atmosphere noticeably relaxed to the extent that Margaret Macdonald became "Bobo": from the cries of "Boo!" in a garden game of hide-and-seek. Bobo was destined to become the Queen's closest woman friend, other than her sister, a figure who will rightly interest posterity though surrounded today with reticence.

Yet there was no hint of this firm future friendship when miniature chairs were set around a miniature play table under the placidly ticking nursery clock, and Elphinstone cousins or the Lascelles boys came to tea or the Allendale children from next door came in to play. The Master of Carnegie, born in 1929, fitted in age between Margaret and Lilibet and Princess Elizabeth would impatiently wait at the lift door whenever another cousin, "Sandy" Ramsay, was coming, filling some impalpable role as an elder brother.

Relatives apart, in the precincts of the small girl's world, there were the ladies and gentlemen of the Household, particularly Lady Helen Graham, the Duchess of York's lady-in-waiting, with her vivacious, birdlike air. Beyond these again, at the fringe of acquaintance, were old ladies to whom one said politely, "How do you do?" There were old gentlemen in wheelchairs, who were presented to her when she was out with Mummy, and there were people more distant still, people unseen, unfathomable, who sent postcards, people who waved from the pavements because they loved one.

At the age of five, Princess Elizabeth rode to the Trooping the Colour ceremony, squeezed in an open carriage with Queen Mary and her parents, raising a hand in response to the cheering crowds as her elders did, and as Alah had taught her to do. That year she was also one of four bridesmaids of her age at the Sussex wedding of Lady Mary Cambridge and Captain Abel Smith. A story told of this period is that, arriving at an exhibition with Queen Mary, the little Princess gleefully exclaimed, "Have all these people come to see me?" and was promptly taken home. But one distrusts the anecdote, as one does the story of the indignant small girl who demanded to have her way with the phrase, "It's Royalty speaking." Lady Helen Graham's closer recollection is of "a lively, trim little figure" who "noticed everything but . . . never thought that she herself was being noticed. This ignorance of her own importance had its drawbacks. She never would understand why photographers, on going to a children's party, would pick her out for their attentions, and she was apt to frown upon them with very obvious disapproval." One morning, in the dining-room overlooking Piccadilly, her parents failed to notice she was standing in the window beyond the lace curtains, and attracting a gathering throng, until she cried, "Mummy, do look—what a lot of people!"

Shortly before Princess Elizabeth's sixth birthday the problem of a governess arose. The nursery staff had meanwhile begun the rudiments of her education and the Duchess herself taught her to read. The Duchess's sister, Lady Rose Leveson-Gower, recommended a young Scotswoman who had taken her own little girl, and so Miss Marion Crawford came to Royal Lodge on—at her own request—

a month's trial. In the autumn she permanently joined the
staff and lessons began in earnest.

When "Crawfie" joined the royal staff she herself was
only twenty-two. Born near Kilmarnock, trained as a
teacher at Moray House College, shocked by some experience of the Edinburgh slums, her crusading sense of voca-
tion had hitherto dwelt more on the poor than the prosperous. She visualized a life work in child psychology, and
had never intended to become a governess, until a chance
holiday invitation to work with Lady Elgin's children and
then the extra session with the Leveson-Gowers drew her
gently on. Conscientious, sparse in build, her hair man-
nishly cropped in the then prevailing style, she made a
virtue of walking three miles from her home to the Elgins,
three further miles to her next class and then three miles
home. Coupled with her evident skill in handling children, this stint considerably impressed the Duke of York
when he heard of it from his sister-in-law. With memories
of his own tutors, either gaunt and solemn or bearded and
lethargic, he wanted his daughter to have the companionship of someone young and energetic. The Duchess of
York put the case to Queen Mary with such finesse that
any opposition was overcome. The Duke and Duchess
were indeed right and Princess Elizabeth soon found in her
youthful Scottish governess a guiding sense of new friendship and fun.

The quiet schoolroom on the top floor of Royal Lodge
overlooked the cool cedars in the garden, and an early
start was made on Barrie's *Peter Pan in Kensington Gardens,* and the farm and animal lore of the *Beacon Readers,*
which few teachers realized were at that time American-

owned. The *Children's Newspaper* entered the house, and
in the *Daily Mirror* the Princess avidly began to follow the
dog, rabbit, and penguin adventures of Pip, Squeak, and
Wilfred. In London, the Duchess arranged that her little
boudoir, off the drawing-room, should be used for lessons. But she was apparently content to "leave the curriculum to Miss Crawford."

"Teach them to write a decent hand, that's all I ask,"
King George V gruffly demanded, on first making Miss
Crawford's acquaintance. Later, the governess went to
Queen Mary with her problems, and the Queen both complimented her on the ingeniously-dovetailed time-table and
suggested some revisions. Should there not perhaps be a
little more time for Bible reading? Would the children
learn poetry by heart? Was it not wonderful memory-train-
ing? Perhaps a little less arithmetic and a little more
history? "Genealogies, historical and dynastic, were very
interesting to children," the Queen sympathetically suggested. So the weekly curriculum came to be amended,
with ninety minutes a week for history to thirty of geography, sixty minutes of grammar being balanced by ninety
minutes of literature, poetry, writing, and composition.

This daily schedule was never arduous. After visiting her
parents' room, Princess Elizabeth sat down to lessons only
from 9.30 to 11. The break for elevenses also began the
period for play in Hamilton Gardens, a shrubby fastness
since swept away and asphalted under the hurrying wheels
of the Hyde Park Corner traffic, but then an enclosure of
smutty laurels, listless rhododendrons, and unclipped
privet that masked a few dejected winding paths. In this
sanctuary the Princess could join in play with the Allendale children and other neighbours. Often her Papa him-

self joined in tournaments of hopscotch, hopping merrily across squares scratched in the gravel, displaying a surprising turn of speed in "tag" or racing for the statue of Byron that served as home. As soon as she was old enough Princess Margaret joined in these scrambles with constant cries of "Wait for me!"

In the nineteen-thirties, when Londoners could usually catch a glimpse of these games from the tops of passing buses, or less effectively through the railings, they came to regard the little Princesses—and politely to disregard them —as a pleasant part of the London scene. With a defence force of detectives and reinforcing nursemaids, Alah had found it impossible to take her charges into the park. More willing to take advantage of natural cover, "Crawfie" could slip out by the side gate with her pupil when the coast was clear, and walk as far as the bridge of the Serpentine or the Round Pond in Kensington Gardens before walking home for the hour before lunch assigned for reading. At Royal Lodge on Saturday morning an hour or so would be spent with a résumé of the week's work or general reading before the Princess went for her riding lesson. "She proved an immensely interesting child to teach, with a high I.Q.," Miss Crawford was to sum up. There was always "a reasonableness rare in anyone so young."

As discipline and attention developed, the afternoons came to be filled, first with the Monday dancing lessons under Madame Vacani, the Tuesday singing lesson at Lady Cavan's, the Wednesday drawing lesson under Miss Cox, the music lesson on Thursday under Miss Mabel Lander. Here a difficulty was experienced: the Princess's memory was so alert that she began playing by ear without learning to read.

But curiously it was from the geography lesson, sand-
wiched almost casually into a mid-week half-hour, that the
Princess first derived some knowledge of her future and so
learned the hardest lesson of all. In the early 'thirties,
while George V reigned, there were no royal tours to bring
the reality of distant lands vividly before a little girl. In
November, 1934, Princess Elizabeth was a leading brides-
maid at the Westminster Abbey wedding of her uncle, the
late Duke of Kent and Princess Marina, and she no doubt
followed their subsequent West Indian cruise by map and
picture. The child knew that the activities of her family,
her uncles, her parents, were somehow connected with the
idea of service to others. She knew that her grandfather
was King, the pomp of a procession, the discipline of his
soldiers, rightfully his, like a king in a picture-book. But
Miss Crawford allowed the postcards and letters that came
from other children, letters written in the Australian out-
back, on African farms or in distant missions, to bring their
own message. As Lady Helen Graham has said, "All breathing loyalty and affection to her as their Princess . . . these
messages from one child to another brought the first direct
revelation to the Princess that she was of importance to
the Empire."

Princess Elizabeth had only just turned nine when King
George V and Queen Mary celebrated their Silver Jubilee
and felt the great surge of national emotion and loyalty
that broke like a wave around the Throne. With her father
and her mother, Lilibet rode in the first of the carriages to
leave Buckingham Palace for St. Paul's, keeping a watchful
eye on little Margaret at her side, and thus she encountered the welcome of the crowds that her grandfather found
"the greatest number of people in the streets that I have

ever seen in my life." Back at the Palace, on the balcony, she was so responsive that she continued to wave when the wearied adults with her could reply no more. Later the Princess accompanied her grandparents on a drive to see the decorations in one of the poorer quarters of London, where every house was decorated with banners and streamers and messages. Touched and yet delighted, the old King must have explained their meaning, speaking in the grave, simple terms that he habitually used with children. And from it Princess Elizabeth must have gleaned that this wild enthusiasm was not only for the King and Queen but also for the Royal Family, not only for the Crown and the royal institution, not only for her Papa and Mummy, but also in some inexplicable, magical degree for herself.

This inaugurated a delightful custom which grandfather and granddaughter clung to for a time when they were in London. The King discovered that from his study window he could look through field-glasses at one of the windows of 145 Piccadilly. Every morning at an agreed time the Princess stood at the window and looked back through binoculars at her grandfather, and so they exchanged their daily greeting.

In 1935 the carefree, unfettered golden age that the young Duke and Duchess of York so ardently desired for their children neared the unclouded zenith of its first decade. The halcyon days were full of activity. "Do you know," Princess Elizabeth exclaimed, wide-eyed one day, "I've been to the Military Tournament *and* the Horse Show *and* the Tattoo!"

At Royal Lodge the Princess had her outdoor cage of blue budgerigars to tend and clean herself. Then there

were the tomtits' feeding-bells to check and replenish, and
the constant cleaning and polishing chores of the little
Welsh house. A strawberry glut brought lessons in jam-
making in the nursery kitchen. There was the corgi,
Dookie, to groom and cherish; and if the dog was out of
harm's way one might have time to lurk in a bush waiting to see a capricious fawn from the Park, who might
or might not consent to appear. Every summer, too,
brought the Glamis holiday with their Strathmore grandparents, Grandpapa, whose whiskers tickled, and Grand-
mama with her stories of "when your Mummy was a little
girl." There was a story both children loved to hear of the
time when the thousand-year-old castle had caught fire and
Mummy had herself been the first to notice the smoke and
telephone the fire brigade.

Glamis always offered exciting things to do, such as
taking the pony down to the station to watch the fish express go through, or begging in the kitchen for newly-
baked cakes. "There were endless dressing-up chests full of
old-fashioned frocks, and tapestries, and hats of other days,
and pieces of silk, and room after room, and passage after
passage, in which to play hide-and-seek and sardines,"
Miss Crawford remembers. Princess Elizabeth committed
the contents of those wonderful chests to memory with
something of Queen Mary's retentive eye. A Tudor dress
of embroidered satin that her mother had once worn for a
charade was so well remembered that it was asked for after
three or four years, and worn at a fancy-dress party given
by Lady Astor.

Lessons continued in some degree even on holiday, and
progress in French was particularly marked when Mlle.
Georgina Guérin was invited to Balmoral. An earlier

teacher had demanded the wearisome writing out of columns of verbs until her exasperated pupil resorted to mutiny. Unable to communicate with her tutor, who persisted in speaking only French, the Princess was driven to the extremity of seizing the inkpot and emptying it over her own golden curls. With Mademoiselle half in hysterics and blue ink dribbling down the Princess's face, the resulting schoolroom scene was unforgettable.

It was true, too, that after learning to swim and losing her timidity of the water, Princess Elizabeth once fell into the lake at Buckingham Palace while looking for a duck's nest. Miss Crawford, hearing a shriek and rushing towards the cries, was confronted with an apparition covered in mud and green duckweed. But on this occasion the Princess hurriedly bathed and changed "before Alah got to hear of it."

Scenes between the two children were similarly neither rare nor numerous, but ran at an average level. Princess Margaret mischievously discovered the pain to be inflicted by tweaking a hat-band until her sister was literally stung to reprisals. "Margaret always wants what I want" was a frequent plaint, and Lilibet's temper, on the few tearful occasions when out of control, took time to simmer down. There is point, however, in the saying that only bored children quarrel and these children were seldom bored.

Playing a game with Queen Mary, when still younger, Princess Elizabeth had been wont to cry, "You mustn't win, Granny. You mustn't win!" Now the impressive dignity of the Queen was sometimes pressed into service, so it is said, for the make-believe of "Presentations."

"Whom have I the pleasure of receiving?" the Queen would inquire, as Lilibet led forward a curtseying Margaret complete with tablecloth train and Red Indian feathers. "Lord Bathtub and Lady Plug," was the reply.

In November, 1935, the Princesses had the fun of dressing up in earnest for the wedding of the Duke and Duchess of Gloucester, at which they both attended the bride. At Christmas, the family was reunited at Sandringham, but the King found the weather too cold to take his granddaughter on their customary stroll around the stables, although she had the amusement of seeing his parrot, Charlotte, at breakfast as usual, delicately treading among the saucers and plates. Yet the atmosphere was heavy. The Duke of Windsor was later to speak of feeling detached and lonely in "this closely knit fabric of family ties" as he watched Elizabeth and Margaret Rose romping around the twenty-foot tree.

On New Year's Eve the household watched the film of *Monte Cristo*, probably the first full-length motion picture which Princess Elizabeth saw. Three weeks later the Princesses were at Royal Lodge when "Crawfie" came, sadly and gently, to tell them that they would never see their grandfather, King George, again.

The grown-ups wondered how the Princesses would face the bereavement forgetting that youth is resilient. The Duke and Duchess of York characteristically sent word to Royal Lodge that the children should not be made too depressed. However Princess Elizabeth now always saw the picture newspapers and to some extent realized the nation's mourning. "Ought we to play?" she asked. Reading of the vigil at the coffin in Sandringham Church and the progress of the gun-carriage from King's Cross Station to Westminster, events may still have seemed remote from the lovable old man who always greeted her hilariously and drew pictures for her on almost any subject she wished.

When the front-page photographs of the lying-in-state in Westminster Hall caught her eye, however, and she read of the endless line of mourning Londoners filing slowly past, she said quietly of her own accord that she would like to go. Dressed in sombre black, she went with her parents and the doors of the hall were momentarily closed for the royal mourners. Asking no questions but tightly clasping her mother's hand, Princess Elizabeth gazed quietly at the catafalque. The harsh outline of the coffin was softened by the draperies of the Royal Standard. The candlelight shone with the superb poetry of state on the Imperial State Crown and the Orb, the tall cross, the bent heads of the four plumed Life Guards, the four Gentlemen at Arms, the four Yeomen of the Guard with their reversed halberds. Afterwards the little girl said, "Everyone was so quiet. As if the King were asleep."

On the day of the funeral Crawfie took the Princess to the station-master's room at Paddington to await the procession, but they arrived over an hour too soon, and the governess sensibly started a game of ticktacktoe to soften the ordeal for a child so young. Then, when the cortege approached to the slow music of the bands, and they moved to the window, while the guncarriage covered with the Union Jack rumbled and grated slowly into sight, the Princess, as Miss Crawford says, "realized what it all meant and her small face quivered." At that very moment, immediately below them, one of the bluejackets marching in the ranks lurched and fainted and the sailors on either side instantly closed ranks and supported him, moving the man forward. Their skill so interested the watching child that she forgot her emotion, and the moment of horror was over. Joining her parents, she found the rest of the day one of rigid duty, an ordeal indeed, but she quietly "meant to go through with it, making no fuss."

Princess Elizabeth had come to know the previous year that her joking, genial Uncle David would one day be King. She had visited his sitting-room at York House, where a portrait of Queen Mary, in white evening gown, with diamonds and the Order of the Garter, hung over the fireplace, and an enormous map of the world, of the Empire, entirely covered one wall. Now Uncle David's frequent visits to 145 Piccadilly and his games with the two little sisters ceased. Visiting Royal Lodge, he brought a puzzling Mrs. Simpson with some friends on one occasion. "Who *is* she?" the Princess asked and was conscious that her uncle made genial plans and then forgot his promises.

Adult events did not unduly disturb the children, however, and with the new reign of Edward VIII normal routine was quickly resumed. Observing six months of Court mourning, Princess Elizabeth could not attend dancing classes. But her swimming lessons under Miss Amy Daly at the Bath Club began around this time.

Having already taught eleven princesses, Miss Daly had her own resourceful methods of engaging royal confidence. On her first visit to the pool Princess Elizabeth found a girl poised on the highest step of the diving-board who, at a word from Miss Daly, expertly performed a swan dive.

The Princess gasped, "Oh, I shall never be able to do that."

"Oh, yes, you will," said Miss Daly. "She is blind and has to trust me absolutely. *You* can see what you're doing."

As soon as his daughter could swim a few strokes, the Duke of York came to the Club to watch her, delighted that she could so easily conquer a medium he had still not mastered when he went to Naval College at Osborne. Princess Margaret was slower and had to be encouraged into the pool with cries of "Don't be a limpet!" But perhaps Princess Elizabeth attributed her buoyancy to the powerful properties of "swimming-cake." Miss Daly gave the children small squares of madeira when she had her tea, unaware of the remarkable and reassuring stories that circulated among her pupils concerning them. One afternoon the Princess arrived with a drawing she had done of herself at diving stance. "But I did it before you gave me the lesson last week," she apologized, "when I didn't know so much about things as I do now." The swimming-cake had been asked for at home.

Queen Mary, having moved into Marlborough House, found solace in organizing Princess Elizabeth's educational excursions, setting aside Monday afternoons to take her to the London Museum, the British Museum, the Wallace Collection and other centres of interest. In August came the usual stay at Glamis and Birkhall, when one of the Elphinstone children gave expert instruction on the wonders of chewing-gum, obtainable from a slot machine at the sleepy and unwatched railway station. There was ample time to place crossed pins, fastened by gum, on the lines and wait until the next train transformed them into scissors.

But with the autumn of King Edward VIII's reign the tempo of visitors to No. 145 quickened. Promoted to luncheon with her parents, Princess Elizabeth was always quick and eager to copy her mother in making herself agreeable and persuading guests to feel at home, but now there seemed more reasons for eating in the nursery or alone with Crawfie. Side by side with the abdication crisis came Mummy's flu, and one could neither meet nor converse so much, so strict was Alah about germs. In the gloom of December, events swirled between Royal Lodge and King Edward's home at Fort Belvedere, while the Princess remained in London. A child's bright eyes noticed the posters, however, and newspapers and radio bulletins could not long be kept from her. It fell to Crawfie to explain that Uncle David had fallen in love with someone England could not accept as their Queen because she had a divorced husband still living. This was a simple moral issue that the Princess could readily accept.

On Thursday, December 10th, soon after ten o'clock, the eleven-month King began signing the fifteen documents of the Instrument of Abdication. As he finished, in the uncharted minutes when she became Heiress Presumptive, Princess Elizabeth was quietly passing from her history lesson to her poetry lesson, according to curriculum. Thursday afternoon usually brought Miss Lander for the music lesson and an old upright piano may have been tinkling in the house at the hour when Queen Mary came to the house to pay her respects to the new Queen Consort and Empress of India.

After the dowager Queen had gone, Miss Crawford was summoned to the new Queen's bedroom to discuss how the children should be told. Perhaps it was helpful that Lilibet had not remained completely in ignorance. "I am afraid there are going to be great changes in our lives. . . . We must take what is coming to us, and make the best of it," said the Queen, so lately the Duchess of York.

Princess Elizabeth, though bewildered, was aware of the making of history. Having occasion to write a note about her swimming lessons, she carefully selected a piece of Buckingham Palace paper and headed it ABDICATION DAY in capital letters. Ten and a half years old, she sufficiently understood the Succession to know why it was that her father had so suddenly become king, but she still did not divine her own future. Although plied with questions, Miss Crawford and Lady Helen Graham were not confronted with that particular problem. The little girls were told that they might have to live in Buckingham Palace and Princess Elizabeth responded with horror, "You mean forever?"

"I was Margaret of York," six-year-old Princess Margaret complained, "and now I'm just Margaret nothing." "Princess Elizabeth," says Lady Helen Graham, "said less because she knew more."

It seems improbable that the King's elder daughter stayed up late to hear her uncle's farewell broadcast at 10 P.M. But a large crowd stood in the lamplight outside 145, cheering from time to time throughout the evening, a tumult that conveyed some faint echo to the children's bedrooms at the back of the house.

When King George VI returned to 145 Piccadilly from his Accession Council, both the children were waiting in the hall and swept him a beautiful curtsey, as Miss Crawford had coached them to do. The King was taken aback and touched, then he stooped and kissed them, and at luncheon there was a great deal of laughter. That Saturday afternoon the Princesses drove with their father to join Queen Mary at Marlborough House, where they could watch his proclamation at St. James's Palace. From the vantage-point of the wardrobe-room, unseen by the crowds,

they had a good view across the roadway of all the colourful pageantry in Friary Court. Queen Mary felt a sense of
relief that all was settled and would not have missed explaining the picturesque elements of the scene to Princess
Elizabeth, the meaning of the supporting Heralds and
Pursuivants, the mace-bearers and State trumpeters. Then
the rich words of Sovereignty, sonorously uttered by Garter
King of Arms, conveyed a special significance to the intent
elder child:

"George the Sixth by the Grace of God, King of the
United Kingdom of Great Britain and Ireland, and of the
British Dominions beyond the Seas, Defender of the Faith,
Emperor of India, to whom we acknowledge all faith and
constant obedience, with all hearty and humble affection,
beseeching God, by whom Kings and Queens do reign. . . ."

Standing at her father's side in the misty December sunlight Princess Elizabeth was also influenced by her mother's
confident religious outlook. "The curious thing is we are
not afraid," the new Queen Consort had written that day
to the Archbishop of Canterbury. "God has enabled us to
face the situation calmly."

The sketchy plans for King Edward VIII's Coronation
on May 12th, 1937, had already decided that the two Princesses should "process" through the Abbey following their
parents. With the same date transferred to King George
VI, the new King and Queen were anxious that Princess
Elizabeth should understand as much as possible of the sacramental and ceremonial aspects of the ritual, but the topic
was deferred until after the Christmas respite at Sandringham. On Christmas Day itself Princess Alexandra of Kent
was born in London and the King's daughters were no
longer alone in the younger generation of princesses.

As if accustomed to a change of Sovereign every twelve-
month, legal pundits now expressed some doubt as to the
position under the Act of Settlement if no son were born
to the King. Would the two girls share the Throne? In the
House of Commons, Sir John Simon, the Home Secretary,
put an end to these speculations by announcing, "In the
event of her father's death, Princess Elizabeth will succeed
to the Throne as sole heir."

The King and Queen moved into Buckingham Palace
on February 15th and the children followed from Royal
Lodge two days later. That first night the wind howled in
the chimneys and the distances appeared vast and awesome.
Lilibet said wistfully that it would be nice to have a secret
tunnel back to 145: her old home was scarcely more remote, perhaps, than her parents' new rooms seemed to be,
in the north corner of the west wing. She herself would
share a bedroom with Bobo. Elizabeth decided at once
that her toy horses, now thirty strong, should be stabled in
the corridor. They were still there on her wedding morning ten years later, so little did she like to see unnecessary
change.

In welcoming the new King, the attitude of the Press
towards his elder daughter, young though she was, was
equally warm with approval. "This little lady has in her
the qualities of greatness," said the *Daily Mail*, and *The
Times* added, "Her self-possessed yet perfectly unspoilt
and childish deportment when she appears with her
mother in public shows that the training of this important
little girl is proceeding on the right lines for the happiness
of the country over which she may one day have to rule."

This praise was verified at an afternoon reception in
March, when Princess Elizabeth helped to receive the

guests, standing with her parents at the top of the Grand
Staircase and walking round the State Rooms afterwards,
talking to the visitors. Not yet afflicted with the shyness
of adolescence, she already showed to an extraordinary degree that she would share her mother's accomplished ease.

Such an event, filling her with party exhilaration, was
a necessary preliminary experience for the Coronation.
From her inexhaustible collections, Queen Mary now
brought a panorama of King George V's Coronation with
all its coloured figures unfolding concertina fashion in a
procession thirty feet long. The Princess soon knew them
by heart. "There's the Lord Mayor carrying the Crystal
Sceptre," she would say. "There's Gold Stick—that will be
Uncle Alge." Her governess also skilfully planned a pre-
Coronation course of reading, ranging from the appropriate journal of the youthful Queen Victoria to H. E.
Marshall's juvenile history, *Our Island Story*. The Princess
thought it a pity that the dramatic challenge to combat
flung down by the armoured King's Champion should have
been discontinued. But unlike most children she read with
compassion rather than mirth of the Champion who had
the misfortune to trip over his sword and fell flat on his
face. "Poor man," she said.

In a fresh and stronger sense, her father, the King, also
helped to shape the early opinions of monarchy that
formed in the young Princess's impressionable mind. The
King took to spending a little time alone with her in his
study early every evening, discussing the day's events, drawing from them some precept or illustration of his own
theories of kingship and perhaps clarifying his own untried
ideas. The weekend after Princess Elizabeth's eleventh
birthday brought a parade of international Boy Scouts at

Windsor, which she watched at His Majesty's side. Two days later she travelled with the King and Queen by royal barge down the Thames to Greenwich, where her father opened the National Maritime Museum. Thus by land and water King George showed his daughter what he had to do, and what the tasks of royalty were in which she must one day play a part. "It is one of my main jobs in life to help others when I can be useful to them," he was later explicitly to sum up in his diary the teachings and the credo that he passed on to the eleven-year-old girl.

One evening, too, the Princess emerged from his study to display with excitement "a very, very special book" he had given her. Bound in beige linen, with her title "Her Royal Highness The Princess Elizabeth" embossed in gold, the volume was her private copy of the illustrated "Order of the Service of the Coronation." The Princess studied it intently . . . the recognition, the symbolism of the swords, the meaning of the white surplice of the Colobium Sindonis. . . . As the days raced towards the final royal rehearsal in the Abbey, which the Princess attended with her sister, every activity appeared to her to take on a Coronation purpose, even to French lessons. It was perhaps the Queen's idea that, on the eve of the festivities, Princess Elizabeth should welcome President Lebrun of France with a little speech in his own language. The speech was learned, and delivered with perfect pronunciation, but not in the parrot fashion that her elders might have expected. The President complimented the young Princess and, to the King's immense pride, she replied impromptu in French without hesitation. "Quite a triumph," her governess thought, "for a girl of eleven."

But it was no less a demonstration of Princess Elizabeth's

responsive Coronation dedication in her own role that she should write an account of the day for her parents. "To Mummy and Papa. In Memory of Their Coronation. From Lilibet." Written in red pencil in a ruled government-issue exercise-book, it has been preserved in the Royal Library at Windsor.

"At five o'clock in the morning I was woken up by the band of the Royal Marines striking up just outside my window. I leapt out of bed and so did Bobo. We put on dressing-gowns and shoes and Bobo made me put on an eiderdown as it was so cold and we crouched in the window looking on to a cold misty morning. There were already some people in the stands and all the time people were coming to them in a stream with occasional pauses in between. Every now and then we were hopping out of bed looking at the bands and the soldiers. At six o'clock Bobo got up and instead of getting up at my usual time I jumped out of bed at half-past seven. When I was going to the bathroom I passed the lift, as usual, and who should walk out but Miss Daly! I was very pleased to see her. . . ."

So began a day of days for a little girl of eleven. In the nursery her cousin and special companion, Margaret Elphinstone, awaited her as a house guest. From Miss Daly on, everyone whom she knew seemed to have been invited to watch "from inside" or to serve and help in some way. When the Princess was having her attendant's dress made for the Gloucesters' wedding, Norman Hartnell, the dressmaker, had thought her more interested in the scintillating cars at her back-door than in the frock. But she was now eighteen months older and almost overawed by the lace and silver splendour of her gown, her purple cloak edged with ermine, appreciating every detail of the ensemble.

"Do you like my silver slippers?" she asked, and lifted her silk skirt to disclose that she was still wearing the short white socks of childhood. Princess Margaret, though on her best behaviour, inevitably caused her sister some concern. "I do hope she won't disgrace us all by falling asleep in the middle," Princess Elizabeth said gravely. "After all, she is very young for a coronation."

But little Margaret had to be nudged only once or twice when playing too loudly with her prayer-books, and capably managed such stressful details as carrying the folded tail of her long cloak over her arm. The children "looked too sweet," Queen Mary wrote, "especially when they put on their coronets." Hand in hand, they preceded Queen Mary in the ceremonial procession from the Abbey. Then the long tumultuous ride on the long route by way of Hyde Park, the repeated appearances on the Palace balcony, the "arranging" for the official photographs which took nearly an hour. Just after seven o'clock Princess Elizabeth looked exhausted and was sent early to bed.

The brilliance of the Coronation in 1937 was one of the last flashes of sunset in a darkening sky. Sixteen days later Mr. Neville Chamberlain was appointed Prime Minister and the age of urgent peace-seeking and appeasement had begun. Hitler had violated the Locarno Treaty by reoccupying the Rhineland and he had intensified the persecution of the Jews, but the era of surprises was, he promised, at an end. The English public had a surprise of a more pleasant nature when Princess Elizabeth appeared unexpectedly at the Coronation Spithead naval review. Uncle "Dickie" Mountbatten, it was noted, bent over and explained the uses of an anchor. With 138 warships mustered in the Solent, the British Navy had tactful reasons for not showing her full strength, but as the creaking royal yacht *Victoria and Albert* steamed up and down the lines, the King and his daughter noticed among the seventeen foreign warships an interesting German small battle cruiser, the *Graf Spee*.

The King and Queen decided that they did not desire Princess Elizabeth's name to be coupled in loyal toasts, since she was still too young to figure in public life, yet there was a sufficient sense of the lowering clouds to make them wish her to share as much as possible in whatever was enjoyably going on. This might mean no more than allowing her to walk on with Princess Margaret, at Windsor, all the way from St. George's Chapel to the Moat Garden, through a crowd of 2,000 companionable people, or in giving her a cake of her own to cut, alongside the cake cut by the King and Queen, at a tea for disabled Servicemen in the Palace Riding School. A blithe forgetfulness was apt to accompany bedtime when the Courts were being held and the children were allowed to watch from their windows, a "fly's-eye view" as Princess Elizabeth called it of gleaming cars and befeathered débutantes. On the night of a State Ball they could discreetly watch the Royal Procession and the commencement of the dancing, hidden and invisible in their pink dressing-gowns, but on tiptoe with excitement, behind an observation grille.

Princess Elizabeth nevertheless continued to do well at her lessons, amply encouraged by the reward of half an hour extra with her pony. Latin was added to the agenda, and the assiduous Miss Crawford was complimented for even giving a walk in the garden, and the names of the flowers, a useful turn. Miss Cox, the drawing mistress,

could report that her pupil was displaying a natural aptitude.

The Princess had posed for Laszlo at the age of seven,
but now displayed alert interest in technicalities. Sitting
for her portrait to Margaret Lindsay Williams, she immediately noticed the turpentine and inquired its use. The
hour-long sittings were passed in telling a serial story of
knights and dragons to Princess Margaret under Alah's
promptings. When Princess Elizabeth faltered, Margaret
or Alah took up the next instalment.

Already, too, the Princess had sat for a bust by Strobl,
the Hungarian sculptor, prepared to pose motionless and
yet grateful to find she could move about, and here the
conversation turned on nationalities. "I am English and
Scottish," she cried one day, with a burst of laughter.
"What a wonderful combination!"

Princess Elizabeth had however no aptitude for knitting
and needlework, and lamented in a letter, "I am being
very slow." Tennis was similarly never to be a strong point.
"The Princess will never succeed unless she forces herself
to run after the ball," her coach asserted. On the other
hand, she gained her certificate for life-saving at the Bath
Club and went on with great verve to win the Children's
Challenge Shield. The young Princess also had a bicycle
and, absurdly, it was national news when she fell off and
grazed her knee. She greatly enjoyed her singing lessons
with Miss Longman, chiefly for the social sense and co-
operative pleasure of participating with other children in
part-songs. The madrigal parties at Windsor were a direct
development of this, some years later.

Queen Elizabeth II indeed can seldom be more fully
occupied than she was as a girl in the transient happy years

from ten to the teens. The Zoo was visited and revisited, as were the Victoria and Albert and the British Museum: "so many different departments," wrote Queen Mary, "that one always finds something fresh." The old Queen now delighted in devising excursions that should be as varied as possible: not merely the Tower of London, Hampton Court, and Greenwich Palace, the National Portrait Gallery and the museums. At the Mount Pleasant Post Office the Princess watched the great rush of letters, and at the Royal Mint she saw the machine that stamped thousands of half-crowns with her father's profile. In the remarkable vaults of the Bank of England she was shown the stacks of bullion and told that she could take away any bar of gold she could carry. This offer, though tempting, was not improvident for the Princess found she could not lift one.

These visits with her grandmother, her governess, and younger sister unfortunately did not give Princess Elizabeth the company of girls of her own age. To allow her social contacts in a wider field, the 1st Buckingham Palace company of Girl Guides was organized. Two Brownies were attached to include Princess Margaret, but the early stages were not altogether successful. As Miss Violet Synge has said, doors were flung wide to the troop by scarlet-coated footmen; and nannies treated the affair as they had the dancing classes, bringing their charges in party frocks with white gloves. Not all the children were as eager to cook sausages on sticks or rough it on the summer-house floor as the Princesses. "*They* won't be able to roll about and get dirty," said Princess Elizabeth, with great scorn, at her first glimpse of the new-comers. There was a scramble game which involved putting all the children's footwear into a heap to be sorted out by their owners, and young Elizabeth discovered to her disgust that some of the children did not know their own shoes. Presently more children of Palace employees and Court officials joined the troop, making a company of twenty Guides and fourteen Brownies, and the sisterhood improved. Any remaining nannies were put to work, proving useful, for example, in emergency first aid. "Are Second Class emergencies *nearly* finished?" complained one nanny, while being vigorously thumped between the shoulder-blades. "It's so very painful, being treated for choking!"

Princess Elizabeth was perhaps already old for her age, accustomed more to the company of adults than other children. A springtime holiday at Eastbourne saw the two Princesses, supposedly incognito, riding ponies on the sands, paddling and building sandcastles, but they did not readily make friends. The bush telegraph was active and everyone on the beach already knew who they were. Weekends at St. Paul's Walden Bury were more successful, and the summer break at Balmoral saw the sisters surrounded by their congenial cousins. With her retentive memory, the Princess could write of her Strathmore grandmother's "delightful bird table . . . my grandfather was collecting all the scraps during lunch and he told me that all sorts of birds came and one day a green woodpecker came. They are very shy birds and rarely come near a house. . . ."

Princess Elizabeth was still only eleven when she attended her first State Opening of Parliament and watched it from the Royal Gallery. At that age, also, she accompanied her mother, the Queen, in many of the official events of the State visit to Scotland, with a sharp eye for the green uniforms and eagle-feathers of the Royal Company of Archers. "The march past of 4,000 soldiers was very tiring," she noted, "because we stood for over an hour and dust was continually blowing in our eyes."

In a sense, Princess Elizabeth was thus prepared for public life at an earlier age than her own children were to be. We find her, aged twelve and two months, taking the salute at a daylight rehearsal of the Aldershot Tattoo before an audience of 5,000 children: a role assumed, it appears, at her own suggestion. She had been allowed to share some of the excitement of the State Visits of King Carol of Rumania and President Lebrun of France, and it was small wonder if spectators at the National Pony Show found that she presented rosettes to the winning riders with great aplomb. On April 6th, 1939, when not yet thirteen, Princess Elizabeth was mentioned in the Court Circular, for the first time during her father's reign, as a guest at the luncheon party given at Windsor Castle for Colonel Beck, the Polish Foreign Minister. One must record it as historically an unpropitious occasion, for as a result of the bilateral agreement made that day Britain was at war with Germany five months later.

The hounds of war, in fact, were baying louder. To encourage others, it was made known that the Princess had been fitted with a gas-mask. A still closer call on the Princess's emotional reserves lay ahead. The visit of the King and Queen to Canada and the U.S.A., which had been under discussion for two years, was now approaching. "If you bring either or both the children with you they will also be very welcome, and I shall try to have one or two Roosevelts of approximately the same age to play with them!" President Roosevelt wrote invitingly to the King.

The King, however, replied, "They are much too young for a strenuous tour."

The departure was fixed for May 5th. The two Princesses and Queen Mary went aboard the royal liner *Empress of Australia* for an exciting inspection and then returned to the quay. The two children had never before been separated from their parents for as long as seven weeks.

"I have my handkerchief," exclaimed Princess Margaret. Queen Mary thought it charming that Princess Elizabeth should quietly add, "To wave, not to cry."

CHAPTER III

TEEN-AGER

IN APRIL, 1939, as she entered her 'teens, Princess Elizabeth had never travelled in a London Underground train and, like many other girls of her age, had not yet met her future husband. Both these events were to be realized in the next three months.

With the departure of their parents to Canada, Princess Margaret insisted that since Papa and Mummy were having an adventure they, too, could have one. Playing up to her sister devotedly, Princess Elizabeth asked servants whether escalators were quite safe for someone aged nine and which was the best way of stepping on or off such an extraordinary moving stair. An unofficial jaunt to the Y.W.C.A. was duly arranged and the great day came.

Scottish-reared Miss Crawford had, in fact, never been on the Underground herself in her life, and Lady Helen Graham, who shared the exploit, was almost equally vague. So the departure was unfortunately, from St. James's Park station (serving the District Line, akin to the subway or the Metro), which involves nothing more subterranean than a stairway, but the thrill of the train rushing out of the tunnel and the sliding doors opening as if by magic was authentic. Then at Charing Cross the children changed to the true deep-level Underground. There came a time, as the train rushed them onward through the tunnel, when a gentleman reading his paper suddenly felt himself the target of all eyes. It took him a few minutes to realize that "two demure children sitting next to him and holding their tickets very ostentatiously in their hands" were the real centre of attraction. Besides, at Tottenham Court Road station, the newspapers had got wind of the adventure and cameramen were waiting. The walk to the Y.W.C.A. had to be completed precipitantly to the flicker of flashbulbs. The adventure could not be repeated.

Princess Elizabeth pored over Underground maps and then over maps of America and perhaps fully realized at last how far away her parents were. The transatlantic telephone could be used only once, as a novelty, and most news came—a week old—by letter. But the time passed. The Music Room in the Palace was so enthusiastically given over to a mixture of Scottish reels and tap-dancing at about this period that the polishers complained the parquets were springing and the dancing classes had to find a stronger floor. Weekends were spent in a frantic spring-clean of the Little House at Royal Lodge.

Then, on June 22nd, the children were taken out by destroyer from Southampton to meet their parents in mid-Channel aboard the *Empress of Britain,* a terrific adventure involving a leap from the battleship to the barge and from the barge to the liner. The two Princesses were thus steeped in nautical atmosphere when they again embarked with the King and Queen on the *Victoria and*

Albert at Weymouth on July 21st. Next day the royal yacht dropped anchor in the River Dart for a visit to the Royal Naval College on the 23rd.

The plan was that the royal party should attend Sunday-morning service in the Chapel, but there had been an outbreak of mumps and chicken-pox, rain threatened, and it was decided that the Princesses should spend the morning at the Captain's House (the pleasant red-brick home of Admiral Sir Frederick Dalrymple-Hamilton, the Captain of the College). Whether by accident or design, Cadet Captain Prince Philip was deputed as Captain's messenger for the day, and the Queen agreed with Lord Louis Mountbatten that he should be excused morning service to help squire the two girls.

Though the story is familiar, Prince Philip as a lad of eighteen perhaps found it harassing to entertain a girl of thirteen and a child of nine. "A fair-haired boy, rather like a Viking, with a sharp face and piercing blue eyes," he nevertheless tried to make himself amusing, joining in playing with Princess Margaret with a set of trains on the floor, but he was in fact, a little nonplussed by the blushing Elizabeth, whom he found shy and reserved. "He could not get a word out of her," a family friend recalls. Then the sun appeared and as a social escape hatch, the blond Cadet Captain suggested a game of croquet with some other cadets. Nevertheless he was relieved when chapel broke and he could relinquish his social duties to others.

Yet the meeting left an impression on both Prince and Princess. "How good he is," Princess Elizabeth afterwards confided. Invited back to lunch on the royal yacht, Prince Philip sat near the Princess and talked and laughed a good deal. In the afternoon they strolled around together, inspecting the College grounds. At dinner aboard the yacht, he discovered that the engaging Princess still observed nursery hours and had not stayed up. On the following day, however, they met again at lunch and tea. "Philip so wanted to make a good impression," a teen-age companion has asserted. Within a year, as the war both severed casual social interchanges and yet sharpened the need for them, the fourteen-year-old girl and the ninteen-year-old midshipman were in full cousinly correspondence.

Princess Elizabeth had always shown a literary bent. If Princess Margaret was the actress of the family, Elizabeth was the author, ready to compose a nursery serial story or record a coronation, quietly pleased when creative thought emerged in a pattern of words, contemplative and not unrelated to the Queen Victoria who published her *Leaves from a Journal.* . . .

History, as Sir Henry Marten has said, can teach one how to write as well as read, "provides an admirable background for English composition . . . gives to the young mind a vast storehouse in which to wander at will . . . a vehicle for the training of the memory, the cultivation of the imagination, the development of balanced judgment. . . . And History may also introduce some of her votaries into the intellectual life." King George VI may not have read these words in Marten's book *On the Teaching of History,* but he had heard of Clarence Henry Marten's quiet scholastic fame as a lecturer to history tutors and schoolmasters, as the staple of history teaching at Eton and as an historian in his own right. A benign round-faced man of sixty-six, Marten had in 1939 been Vice-Provost of Eton for eight years, and the King decided that

he should be asked to give Princess Elizabeth extra tutor-
ship in constitutional history.

The Princess was as nervous as any new boy, when she
first entered the Vice-Provost's study in Eton College and
gasped in admiration at the piles of books, volumes of
every size, overflowing from shelves to chairs and stacked
on the floor. He began Princess Elizabeth gently, it appears, with a game of royal lotto. There were coloured
counters, red for Kings, blue for Queens, brown for Princes
and other colours for their kinsfolk, which if fitted into
place in a jigsaw pattern represented the relationship and
lineage of the Royal Family through the centuries. Soon
Marten was taking her in history twice a week, amid the
clatter of schoolboy footsteps at Eton, or at Windsor or
the Palace, whichever was most convenient. The Princess used a set of green Eton notebooks which she kept in
good order, learning the usage of abbreviations and tidily
indenting her headings and sub-headings. So began the
strong and dynamic flow of a sustaining interest that was
to carry her forward in calm as the world turned from
peace to war.

Miss Crawford was hurriedly recalled from holiday and
the household in Scotland settled down to a new routine.
Alah made sure that the girls were ready for lessons punctually at 9.30, and the usual break at 11 brought the
opportunity for a brisk walk or pony ride through the
familiar pines along Glen Muick. As time developed,
the Newfoundland lumberjacks' camp near Ballater became a popular target for excursions, where brawny men
in colourful shirts would sometimes pause with their
axes and grin as the little girls passed. Princess Elizabeth
detected three or four Red Indians and made a point of

looking out for them. Meanwhile, Marten's history papers and notes arrived to occupy her usual afternoon attention. The Princess dutifully prepared essays each week to be posted back to him for correction. Sometimes her tutor ringed a word for misspelling, or a Z indicated that a new paragraph was needed. An N—for nonsense—was rare.

Meanwhile, it became Miss Crawford's task to discuss the daily war news with her protégée and explain events. The mention of any naval vessel would immediately see the Princess identifying it in *Jane's Fighting Ships* if, indeed, she were not familiar with it already. In mid-October the radio announcement of the sinking of the *Royal Oak* caused the young girl to stand in horror, "her eyes blazing with anger," as Crawfie recalled long after. These were the terrible truths of war. "What dreadful things have been happening," the Princess wrote sadly. On the other hand, this was the period of the "phoney war," and since the air-raid alarm sirens seemed to sound in London when nothing happened, the Princess could laugh at a line she had just read in Milton, "Blest pair of sirens, pledges of heaven's joy."

When evacuees from Glasgow, children with their mothers, moved into the Balmoral estate, a Red Cross sewing party was organized one afternoon a week in the Birkhall schoolroom. The Princesses helped Alah as hostess, tended the large horn gramophone as the ladies sewed, then handed round tea and cake and joined in the talk, becoming familiar with the activities of sons or husbands in the Forces. It would have surprised these men had they known, as they drilled in barrack squares or served at sea, that the Princess asked after them, and prided herself on knowing their news. Meanwhile, Princess Margaret's fa-

vourite musical choice of "Thy Tiny Hand is Frozen" became extremely apt as the winter cold intensified and the
schoolroom chilled despite the best efforts of the tiny wood
stove. The November frosts and December snow created
a Scotland the Princesses had never known. Though the
Birkhall fireplaces were well fuelled, face-cloths became
sheets of ice in the bedrooms.

The local Girl Guides company was so considerably
expanded by evacuees that meetings had to take place in
the village hall. Helping to organize outings and cinema
shows, Princess Elizabeth could feel she was doing her
share. On wet afternoons a local man with a projector put
on some old Laurel and Hardy films. When the weather
cleared hikes with the Glasgow children, who had been
accustomed to streets all their lives, helped to lessen their
metropolitan fear of the woods. Rehearsals began for a
Christmas play, *The Christmas Child*, with the Birkhall
schoolchildren, and Princess Elizabeth was delighted to
find herself cast as one of the Three Kings. Since the Princess was also wearing bands on her teeth at this time,
entailing a visit to the dentist's, an expedition into Aber-
deen was an opportunity to buy cellophane for the stage
jewels and Woolworth's was visited for Christmas gifts.
Then one of the schoolchildren unluckily caught mumps
and the play was cancelled.

To their joy, however, the Princesses heard that they
were to spend Christmas at Sandringham as usual. Although the house was admittedly exposed to the East Coast
visit of German reconnaissance planes, the inactivity of
the "phoney war" justified the risk. At the "Big House"
Princess Elizabeth found a new pony, Pussyfoot, awaiting
her, and the children in turn surprised and delighted their

parents by singing French duets, a surprise carefully prepared in conspiracy with Mrs. Montaudon-Smith, who had
lately taken charge of their French lessons in Scotland. On
Christmas afternoon the Princesses heard their father give
the first of his Christmas broadcasts and speak the lines of
poetry in which he found faith could be strengthened in
the face of the dark and unknown future. ". . . put your
hand into the Hand of God. That shall be to you better
than light, and safer than a known way."

"May that Almighty Hand guide and uphold us all,"
the King concluded, and quietly his daughter said,
"Amen."

The children did not return to Scotland. The Princess,
growing up now, celebrated her fourteenth birthday at
Royal Lodge, and members of the Household began to
address her as "Ma'am." Schoolroom routine and the regular visits to Marten continued, but on May 12th the full
force of the German paratroop attack was unleashed on
Holland. Following a prearranged plan, the Queen immediately telephoned Royal Lodge and directed that the
Princesses should be taken at once to Windsor Castle.
"Evacuated to a house in the country," as it was said, they
were to remain in residence for the duration.

The furnishings of the Castle had been partly disman-
tled. The choice pictures had been removed, leaving their
vague outlines on the walls. Glass-fronted cupboards had
been turned to the wall; chandeliers had been banished;
many walls were sandbagged, and some of the pieces of
furniture were covered in dust-sheets summer and winter,
producing a ghostly and mournful effect on the inhab-
itants. The choicer pieces of the Regalia reposed in the

cellars, where Princess Elizabeth was once shown her mother's crown, safe in an old hatbox stuffed with newspaper. The Princesses were housed in their usual rooms in the Lancaster Tower, which boasted the immensely thick walls and winding stairway built under Henry VII and still seemed to have plumbing and heating in keeping.

With Lord Wigram, aged sixty-seven, Brigadier-General Sir Hill Child, aged sixty, and others, the Princesses were surrounded by elderly adults. But presently a company of Grenadier Guards arrived and a group of young officers often lunched or came to tea with Princess Elizabeth and Crawfie.

Thus at the age of fourteen the Princess again found herself playing hostess as she had at Birkhall, supervising the placing and pouring tea. Her elders admired her tactful skill as a conversationalist acquired by watching her parents. A local group that also interested the Princess was the light anti-aircraft battery whom she named the Bofors boys. When they sent her a Christmas card, she was charmed, and specially mentioned it in her family letters.

Princess Elizabeth's essential stability and calmness of character carried her smoothly through the difficulties of adolescence. She did, however, develop a fetish about tidiness and would climb out of bed to set her shoes straight or to refold garments on a chair. Princess Margaret helped to laugh her out of this with a hilarious imitation of her preparations for slumber. Yet was it surprising for the methodical, disciplined daughter of the King to show this compulsive wish to be orderly in a disordered world?

When an air-raid alert sounded the Princess refused at

first to descend to the shelter down in the dungeons without getting dressed. Then the two girls were given siren
suits and little cases in which they could keep their most
treasured possessions ready packed, including their diaries
—each with separate lock and key—which they conscientiously entered up every night. Actually in those early
months after the evacuation of Dunkirk the air-raid warn-
ings were not too numerous. When the wail of the Windsor sirens announced a stray enemy daylight plane, the
Princesses sometimes took shelter in one of George III's
pebble-lined Gothic catacombs in the hillside or else
walked to the comparative safety of the nearest summer-
house. In all levels of society, much of the ordinary summer life of Britain went on as usual in 1940. There was,
as King George VI's biographer has said, "a moment of
dread quiet." Whenever possible, the King and Queen
made a weekend visit to Windsor, to be eagerly met at one
of the gates by the Princesses, waiting with their ponies
and dogs.

With head bent over her history books, Princess Elizabeth could sometimes hear the rattle of gunfire at the
shooting-range in the gardens. The personal perils of invasion were so real that the King and members of the family practised with pistols and tommy-guns. But by the time
the King gave his elder daughter lessons in rifle-shooting
the worst was over.

The question of sending the Princesses to Canada in an
emergency was discussed and dismissed. Their departure
would have an adverse effect on public morale. Then too,
the Queen said, "'They could not go without me and I
could not possibly leave the King." Desultory gardening
expeditions were made to Royal Lodge, where the King

instructed his daughters in the stirrup-pump and fire-fighting drill. Practising in their Fire Prevention Unit, King George and his daughters addressed one another as Numbers One, Two and Three, and sprayed water with great hilarity. All the same, this game typified the nation's defiant attitude. "The children used to be swimming about in the pool with the drone of enemy planes over-head," the Queen said later. Princess Elizabeth, however, expressed concern lest she was being "too happy." She spent odd moments attempting to master those wilful knit-ting-needles of hers, knitting hospital bedsocks or woollen headgear for Civil Defence personnel.

The official evacuation of schoolchildren from London brought a quota of evacuees to Windsor. These were quickly welcomed into the Guide company and made to feel at home, and the old cry of "Wait for me, Lilibet," was now to be heard in all sorts of accents and especially in Cockney.

The King, in spite of his preoccupations, resumed the lessons in statecraft that he had begun before the war. During one of these afternoons at Royal Lodge, Mrs. Sheridan watched father and daughter together while the King dealt with one of his red dispatch boxes. "He drew Princess Elizabeth's attention to a certain document and explained certain matters to her very earnestly." The King also desired his daughters to meet the leading personalities of the day, and when Mrs. Roosevelt visited London both the Princesses went to the Palace in spite of the hazard.

While Queen Mary was at Badminton, Princess Eliza-beth went scavenging for old tins for scrap with her East End friends, scouring a coppice for firewood or doing her share of the greasy washing-up after camp. She felt keenly the loneliness of these waifs away from their parents, and when London was raided she tried her best to comfort them. A restless conviction that she was not doing her bit made her suggest that she should broadcast to the children of the Empire. Families everywhere were torn apart, children were in need of reassurance. The Princess argued so persuasively that she won her father's permission for the broadcast.

She wrote the first draft script herself and arranged for ten-year-old Princess Margaret to join in saying "Good night, children," so that her sister should not feel left out. She dutifully spent an hour or so every day, rehearsing her breathing and phrasing. Listening to one of the engineers' final rehearsals from outside his study, the King was struck by the microphone resemblance to the Queen and burst in saying excitedly, "She sounds exactly like her!" Actually the Princess experienced some nervous difficulty with the tempo of her delivery, and the Queen sat at her side during the transmission beating out the time with her hand.

The broadcast proved to be timely, given as it was in Children's Hour six days after a force of 450 enemy planes had attacked London. "I can truthfully say to you that all we children at home are full of cheerfulness and courage. We are trying to do all we can to help our gallant sailors, soldiers and airmen, and we are trying, too, to bear our own share of the danger and sadness of war. We know, every one of us, that in the end all will be well." So said the Princess before adding her impromptu, "Now come on, Margaret."

In Badminton, Queen Mary was moved to tears as she listened. Five thousand miles away the South African novelist, Sarah Gertrude Millin, noted, "It was perfectly done. If there are still queens in the world a generation hence, this child will be a good queen."

The nightmare proximity of invasion receded and the future Queen could continue her studies of somewhat earlier history with a more tranquil heart. She began attending history lectures at Eton under Mr. Marten and got to know a group of Eton boys, some of whom subsequently joined her Windsor madrigal group. With the long winter nights to be spent behind blackout curtains, and the continual tension of the air-raid sirens, the need of an evening diversion became self-evident. So rehearsals of the play, *The Christmas Child*, which had met such an inglorious end at Birkhall, were started again. The two girls now went to bed nightly in the reinforced air-raid shelter, and if an urgent red warning sent them down earlier, they passed the time studying their lines. Fortunately the actual performance at the Castle—staged in the medieval atmosphere of St. George's Hall—was uninterrupted by enemy alerts. For the first time, Princess Elizabeth wore a crown, a make-believe crown left over, perhaps, from an Edwardian fancy-dress ball, and members of the audience thought it a pleasant portent that she wore it with humility, carrying gifts of frankincense and myrrh, as one of the Three Kings.

The shepherds were schoolboys with scarves for turbans. Princess Margaret played the Little Child. No public whisper of this performance had, of course, been permitted, but the long and spacious hall was half full, with relatives and friends of the performers, Castle staff and others. The audience was delighted with the production, the King so touched by the pathos and youthful charm of the performers that he wrote with emotion, "I cried all the way through."

The collection plate netted thirty pounds for charity. Thereupon Princess Margaret was convinced that if seats could be priced and sold, the proceeds for charity would be even higher, and a summer concert for charity, with piano duets and tap-dancing, was undertaken. Princess Elizabeth was shocked at a proposed admission of seven shillings and sixpence. "No one will pay that to look at us!" she said in astonishment. But subsequently this price was fixed for front seats at the Windsor pantomimes, and *Cinderella* (1941), *The Sleeping Beauty* (1942), *Aladdin* (1943), and *Old Mother Red Riding Boots* (1944) raised a total of £850 for the Queen's Wool Fund.

These Christmas shows were, of course, rare interludes of excitement in the seclusion and settled rhythm of the early war years, years so favourable to study and the quiet, unforced flowering of character, but it must not be thought that Princess Elizabeth was "a war-time prisoner of Windsor," as some have suggested. The opening of 1941 found her with her parents cushioned in deep snow at Appleton House. (Here she was much concerned with persuading her father to send Prince Philip a Christmas card through speedy diplomatic channels in return for one he had sent her from Athens.)

In high summer, Mr. MacKenzie King, the Canadian Prime Minister, gives us another picture from Balmoral, where he first met the Princesses at the Queen's little two-room picnic cottage on the moors. "They had arranged the table inside with lettuce leaves for decoration. They were quite pleased with everything they had done to make things look nice. There were no servants." And later he found Princess Elizabeth, now fifteen years old, "very sweet in the way she talked . . . very natural in some further conversation we had together."

Noticeably, the Princess did not intrude Canadian affairs as a topic, though her studies with her tutor that term appear to have been devoted to "The Evolution of a Self-Governing Dominion." She had now read Professor Trevelyan's *English Social History* and progressed during a term devoted to "The Colonies" to reading Lord Elton's *Imperial Commonwealth*. On occasion the volumes prescribed by the Vice-Provost of Eton were so exacting that copies could be found, in fine old bindings, only in the House of Commons library. Mr. Marten would sometimes clap a book for dust, explaining that it was a dusty subject. He seized quickly on anything that could provide an object lesson. A swarm of bees near the library window at Windsor made him digress into the laws of ownership. "If they have any owners, those owners have rights, and so has the owner of the property on which they swarm. I think we ought to know about those rights . . ." he would begin, gently.

Later the Princess devoted a term to the Indian problem and another to studying "the national exchequer in war and peace." Step by step she was taken through the liberties and the laws of England, through the growth and apparatus of the Monarchy and its relationship to the Church, Parliament, the Cabinet, and the evolution of the British Commonwealth.

However she also developed an extensive interest in her father's racing affairs, especially when the colt Big Game emerged as an unbeatable two-year-old in every race he ran.

Again, though the Princess was not green-fingered, she took it for granted that she should help the gardeners during the manpower shortage, picking peas and helping to salvage the plum crop when branches were breaking under the weight.

Meanwhile, Miss Lander, whom the Princess nicknamed "Goosey," came for piano lessons, and at fifteen Princess Elizabeth was playing Beethoven, Chopin and Debussy "very well . . . with real musical feeling." Mrs. Montaudon-Smith ("Monty") still came for French; and the German attack upon Russia, the opening of the Libya campaign, and the attack on Pearl Harbor caused Miss Crawford to unroll new sets of maps to help Mr. Marten in his lectures on current affairs.

The Provost alone lacked a nickname. But the Princess knew he had a sweet tooth and affectionately sent him two pounds of honey a week throughout the war. Perhaps on one occasion she took him a cake she had baked herself, for Thursday afternoon was devoted to culinary instruction, in a class of twelve for the Guides' cooking badge. The Princess had gained her Guides' Proficiency Badge, having passed in first aid, thrift, music, map-reading, swimming, and as an interpreter in French. "Cook, Needlewoman and Child Nurse are holding me up a bit," she wrote with apologies to her Guide captain.

As the sixteenth anniversary of her birthday approached, the Rev. Stafford Crawley, Canon of St. George's Chapel, also prepared the Princess Elizabeth for her confirmation. This renewal of baptismal vows by the King's elder daughter was approached with great reverence, and Dr. Cosmo Lang, the Archbishop of Canterbury, visited the Princess on February 28th, the eve of the ceremony. He had "a

full talk with the little lady alone," as he recorded, "and
though naturally not very communicative, she showed real
intelligence and understanding. I thought much, but said
little, of the responsibilities which may be awaiting her in
the future. The Confirmation itself was very simple—in
the ugly private Chapel."

But the Archbishop managed to convey the thoughts he
had left unspoken. "I'll have to try to be good, won't I?"
said the Princess to a friend, in an impulsive moment
reminiscent of the young Queen Victoria. With memories
of her own trepidation on such a day, Queen Mary
motored from Badminton and noted that her granddaughter "looked so nice in white with a small veil and was quite
composed." The old Archbishop, who was making the
confirmation the last official act of his career, added that
there were "only a few relations and friends and the boys
of St. George's choir present. . . . My address was just what
I have so often given in country churches."

It is notable that amid the plethora of royal photographs, no photograph of Princess Elizabeth dressed for
this ceremony has ever been released by the Palace, so
deeply personal and sacred was her Confirmation held to
be.

CHAPTER IV

GROWING UP

Two months before her sixteenth birthday in 1942 the King formally appointed Princess Elizabeth a Colonel in the Grenadier Guards. This was a matter of great pride and pleasure to her. Versed in regimental lore and sharing her father's interest in decorations, including his extraordinary ability to read medals and ribbons at a glance, she realized that the appointment also conveyed her father's esteem, a personal avowal of faith in her ability. On her birthday itself she inspected the regiment at a review of 600 men at Windsor. The commanding officers took great pains to render her due honour, sending small detachments to represent every battalion, even including units serving with the Armoured Division and members of the Old Comrades Association. A photograph has caught the moment of the parade when the regiment accorded her three cheers: the Princess stands rigidly to attention on the dais at her father's side, her figure still plumpish and juvenile in pleated skirt and woollen jacket, but her features taut, every muscle tense as if seeking to embody all the discipline of regimental tradition in her small person.

That afternoon the Princess donned her Girl Guides uniform and went to the Windsor Labour Exchange to register under the preliminary youth registration scheme of the National Service Act. She posed with pen and official form pad, smiling for the cameras; she indicated the Girl Guides as her requisite pre-Service training. Perhaps she noticed sceptical as well as admiring smiles among the other girls of her age-group who had waited to see her. From that moment, in any event she agitated to be allowed to join one of the women's services.

She could undeniably argue that many of her own friends were already going. She could plead with her father that Lady Patricia Mountbatten had become an officer in the Wrens and that her cousin Lady Mary Cambridge was serving in the V.A.D.s and, moreover, in one of the worst-blitzed parts of London. "Look what Mary's doing," she urged.

More aware of the value of her survival as heiress presumptive than she was herself, the King no doubt promised to think about it and adopted a convenient attitude of parental vagueness. A secretary tactfully put before the impatient Princess the newspaper reminder of "a high Court official" that "the Princess really became liable for national service, of a very special kind, at her birth." Currently, however, this was no more than working with a W.I. group or leading a war savings week with a pound note given her for the occasion. And, as time went on, war casualties within the family heightened her impatience. Her Bowes-Lyon cousin, the Master of Glamis, was reported "missing, believed killed" in the Middle East, and

Andrew Elphinstone was already a prisoner-of-war at Oflag 4C. Lord Louis Mountbatten had encountered a narrow escape when his destroyer *Kelly* sank under him in the Mediterranean, and his experience heightened Princess Elizabeth's concern for Prince Philip, on destroyer patrol in the North Sea. The Royal Family gathered at Windsor for the christening of Prince Michael of Kent on August 4th, the Queen's birthday, and three weeks later Princess Elizabeth was at Balmoral when she had to brace herself to the tragic news of the death of the Duke of Kent, her popular "Uncle Georgie."

"I ought to do more," she said continually. With immense zeal but little guidance, untrained except by her own observation, the Princess interested herself so thoroughly in her Grenadiers that she perhaps taxed the ingenuity of her brother officers to devise duties suitable to so young a colonel. The Princess was exacting, her unassailable standards as demanding as those she imposed on herself, and at first, in pursuing her imaginary ideal of what a colonel should be, she felt it just to express criticism as well as praise. After her comment to one young man at inspection, delivered with cold glance and peremptory tone, a major diplomatically hinted to one of her elders, "You should perhaps tell the Princess quietly that the first requisite of a really good officer is to be able to temper justice with mercy." After that, there were no longer wry smiles in the mess, for the Princess was quick to learn.

A new outlet for her high spirits also developed in the Sea Rangers' camp beside the quiet lake at Frogmore, where the Princess learned to handle a sail, exercised her skill at the tiller and earned a bosun's badge. For a time she slept with other girls under canvas, but she seemed to keep finding good reasons for not doing so, and so was relieved when seniority enabled her to sleep in a summer-house, incidentally the selfsame one used by Queen Victoria in her old age. But the camaraderie of the early-morning breakfasts, cooked in the open air with her contemporaries, was invaluable, and the night camps continued until the "buzz bombs" of 1944 made it difficult for girls to sleep away from their homes. The Princess herself was cooking sausages one morning when she saw one of these strange aircraft coming over. She sprawled flat with drilled promptitude. The thing trundled overhead, then cut out and presently exploded on the Windsor racecourse. After that camping had to be staged within close reach of a slit trench.

Indoors at Windsor, when gunfire sounded, the Princess always wanted to see what was going on and often had to be pulled away from a dangerous window. Yet she showed signs of strain, too, as she listened to the radio bulletins. The cost of the desert victories and the Italian offensive especially shadowed the young Princess with the harsh facts of war. When from time to time any of the young officers whom she had known at Windsor was listed as killed, she took it upon herself to write a letter to the bereaved mother, giving her appreciative memories of him at Windsor. It seemed to the Princess Elizabeth the least she could do.

In June, 1943, the King left Britain to visit his troops in North Africa and his much-bombed people in Malta. In delegating temporary authority to five Counsellors of State, it became apparent that, under the Regency Act of 1937, his elder daughter was debarred and could not serve as a Counsellor of State until she was twenty-one. When Parliament reassembled he requested that the Regency Act should be amended to allow Princess Elizabeth to become eligible as a Counsellor of State at eighteen, "in order that she should have every opportunity of gaining experience in the duties which would fall upon her in the event of her acceding to the Throne." A Bill to amend the 1937 Act was promptly introduced, passing without opposition through both Houses and on November 11th, 1943, the provision that "The Heir Apparent or Heir Presumptive to the Throne, if not under 18 years, should not be disqualified from being a Counsellor of State by reason only of his not being of full age," became law.

Now, however, the new Regency Act sparked off the mistaken idea that she came of age at eighteen and the equal misapprehension that she might be created "Princess of Wales" on that day. This agitation disturbed the King. "How could I create Lilibet the Princess of Wales," he wrote to Queen Mary at Badminton, "when it is the recognized title of the wife of the Prince of Wales? Her own name is so nice . . . what name would she be called by when she marries, I want to know?"

All these legalisms were in the air when, in point of fact, the whole question of Princess Elizabeth's future was passing into a more intimate domestic sphere. "Did you have a happy Christmas?" Princess Margaret wrote to a friend. "We did. Philip came!" Indeed Prince Philip was at Windsor as early as October 1941, when he had just returned from Cape Town, travelling, oddly enough, in those days of war-time convoys, by way of Nova Scotia. From then on he visited Windsor ever more frequently when on shore leave and wrote to Princess Elizabeth with new warmth after his destroyer *Wallace* was sent to Malta. By the end of 1943, when he was certainly one of the most absorbed spectators at the Windsor pantomime, the Royal Family understood the situation and had agreed to ignore it.

"She is too young," the King wrote to keep Queen Mary informed. "She has never met any young men of her own age." Although the King liked Prince Philip and found him intelligent, with a good sense of humour and sound principles, he told the young man that he "had better not think any more about it for the present."

Yet the world was opening up at last for Princess Elizabeth as she stepped from the schoolroom. Her eighteenth birthday again saw a military celebration, and the Changing of the Guard at Windsor was made the occasion of a ceremony for the presentation of the Colonel's Standard. Queen Mary, the Duke and Duchess of Gloucester, the Duchess of Kent, the Princess Royal, and Earl Harewood attended the family lunch that followed. Next, on May 1st, a meeting of Dominion Prime Ministers in London concluded with a dinner at Buckingham Palace, and Princess Elizabeth attended, almost as a symbol of coming out, her first official dinner. She was seated between General Smuts of South Africa and Mr. Mackenzie King of Canada. The latter noted her as "very natural, not in the least shy. Looked very pretty and very happy and graceful." But even now Princess Elizabeth could not persuade her father to allow her to join the Services.

She was, however, given her own lady-in-waiting, Lady Mary Strachey, to act as secretary and stage-manage her first public activities. Now too, the Princess Royal's old sitting-room at Windsor was rearranged as a sitting-room for the Heiress Presumptive. Soon after this Princess Elizabeth accepted an invitation to become president of the National Society for the Prevention of Cruelty to Children, and her first public visit to the City of London on May 31st, saw her installed as the new N.S.P.C.C. President at the Mansion House. "I would like you to know that the all-important work which the Society has done and is doing for the children of this country lies very near my heart. . . . I trust that in the days to come we may hope that every child's life may be a free and happy one." Such was the first speech of a future Queen.

It was, moreover, an ecstatically happy Princess who moved about London in that sunny summer of liberation. She was in love and thought that no one knew her secret; she was mistress of her own affairs and found great joy in at last fully giving her services to the community she was dedicated to serve. A new tide of correspondence flowed across her desk, from hospitals and orphanages, from charitable societies and benevolent institutions, from such good causes as the Student Nurses' Association, the Life Saving Society, the Royal Amateur Orchestral Society, the Red Cross societies of Australia and Canada and many others. Her presidential speeches at this stage were entirely her own: she would spend long, quiet hours revising and practising aloud. A film of her activities, *Heir to the Throne,* was made that summer and the Princess delighted in acting a scene at her desk. Unlike her mother and sister, she insisted on wearing full make-up. "We look like wan ghosts," complained Princess Margaret later. "How right you were!"

There were visits to bomber stations, one day with her parents to a British base, and, with Princess Margaret included in the party, a visit to an American base the next. Space limitations in the tiny newspapers of those war days sometimes caused Princess Margaret to be cut out of the photographs. This so annoyed Princess Elizabeth and so mortified her sister that a round robin was sent to newspaper editors, "Please do NOT cut Princess Margaret out of pictures!"

Perhaps it was just as well on the day of her first official speech that Princess Elizabeth did not know that the possibility of her succession had suddenly been placed before the King. His Majesty was eager to watch the attack on the Normandy beaches in a joint expedition with Mr. Churchill, but the hazards of this enterprise appalled the King's Private Secretary, Sir Alan Lascelles. By way of dissuasion, Sir Alan quietly asked the King whether instructions would be prepared to advise Princess Elizabeth on the choice of her first Prime Minister if the King and Mr. Churchill were killed simultaneously. The King slept on his beach-head plan and next day asked Mr. Churchill to reconsider it. The plan was called off.

By July 23rd, however, King George felt the situation on the southern front so improved that he was able to visit his armies in Italy without undue constitutional risk, and on that day Princess Elizabeth first assumed royal functions—with the Queen, the Duke of Gloucester, the Princess Royal and Prince Arthur of Connaught—as a Counsellor of State. The King was absent for barely two weeks and the legal business of the Counsellors is narrowly defined, but for the first time the Princess had her hand on the wheel of State. Among the papers she signed were documents concerned with a murder reprieve, a case confronting her sharply with sordid reality. "What makes people do such things?" she asked. "One ought to know. I have so much to learn about people."

But the year was filled with many new lessons for the Princess. During the Balmoral holiday she also visited Edinburgh for her first official ceremony in Scotland, receiving purses for a Y.M.C.A. appeal fund. On December 1st, unannounced amid the secrecies and censorship of war, she went to the shipyard of John Brown and Co. on Clydebank to launch the battleship *Vanguard*, then the newest and most powerful capital ship in the world. Here were no crowds of juveniles or housewives or polite committee women to cheer her this time, but grimy workmen with their broad, rough jokes. "May God bless her and all who sail her," said the Princess, in the traditional manner, unaware that she was launching the ship in which she was later to sail for her first visit to one of the great territories of the British Commonwealth.

In 1945, King George VI felt he could now allow his elder daughter to join one of the Services, and in March she was granted an honorary commission as Second Subaltern in the Auxiliary Territorial Service. This was a popular move. A newspaper was able to announce excitedly "Second Subaltern Elizabeth Windsor, A.T.S., Heir to the Throne of England, will be plain ma'am to her subordinates and will share sleeping-quarters with her sister officers. She will sleep in a camp bed like any other A.T.S. girl." Although this was wide of the mark, the Princess's life was made as much like that of a junior officer as possible. Her Company commander, Commandant V. E. M. Wellesley, briskly arrived at Windsor to welcome her to the Service and motor her to the No. 1. Mechanical Transport Training Centre at Camberley, but at the depot the Princess found a car awaiting her, jacked up, its wheels off, and she was promptly pitched into the N.C.O.'s course in the theory and practice of heavy mechanics. She could not then drive a car, and the course was designed to take her from the first lecture on the Highway Code to night driving and the repair of heavy trucks.

The Princess did not sleep in barracks, but returned to Windsor every night, and at dinner sometimes talked of nothing but spark plugs. The arrival of her uniform was a matter of pride, a sign that she was able to do what other ordinary girls of her age had to do. Within a few days she was hustled into the driving-seat of a Bedford truck and ordered to drive it along a private Army road. Her instructors had been told to treat her "like any other." And within a few weeks the Princess was driving the fifth truck in a learner's convoy through the narrow streets of a royal and ancient borough that had never anticipated this new and mobile form of visiting royalty. The engine of the front truck stalled, the convoy was held up, and this meant a difficult start on a slope. But the Princess managed it splendidly.

Later she progressed to a Wolseley staff car and finally to a large field ambulance. Her colonelcy was, of course, waived and the Princess also had to spend time in the instruction pits and at the repair benches, and she faced the same discipline as the corporals and sergeants in the workshop with her. A visit of inspection by Queen Mary opened her eyes to some of the absurdities of Army spit and polish. "You have no idea what a business it has been—everyone working so hard," was her private comment. "Now I real-

ize what must happen when Papa and Mummy go anywhere. It's something I'll never forget."

Soon Princess Elizabeth was driving Commandant Wellesley to Camberley. The mornings were devoted to driving practice on the roads and to lectures on maintenance
and servicing, map-reading and kindred subjects. The
afternoon brought practical instruction, when the Princess
would find herself with oil-smeared hands changing a
wheel or putting in a new spark plug. Simultaneously she
attended lectures in administration and military law and
went through the routine of the mess, taking her turn as
a duty officer. On the day of her last test the King and
Queen and Princess Margaret arrived and found her with
smudged face under a car, "very grave and determined to
get good marks," as Miss Crawford noted. The King decided to watch other teams of girls at work, and left her
to it, but presently he returned and remarked jocularly,
"What, not got it going yet?" Nor was this the end of his
teasing, for when Princess Elizabeth clambered into the
driving-seat and switched on the ignition, nothing happened. The King then disclosed that he had surreptitiously
removed the distributor.

Before the war ended, it is said, the Princess trium-
phantly drove a heavy truck up to London through the
blackout and into the courtyard of Buckingham Palace.
Commandant Wellesley was able to report: "Her Royal
Highness is a very good and extremely considerate driver."
In reality the "heavy truck" was a staff car and the journey
was made in daylight. Undue exaggeration of moderate
achievements was to plague Elizabeth the popular Princess
again and again.

The world was widening now and presently Elizabeth's

A.T.S. training became but a part of her activities, although it occupied the major part of her attention for a year to complete the full course. Some of her own personal enjoyments had to go by the board: arriving for a music lesson Miss Lander would be greeted with the regretful cry, "Oh, Goosey, I haven't got on at all!"

As the nineteenth birthday of Her Royal Highness approached, an additional lady-in-waiting was appointed to enhance the dignity of her establishment, and incidentally, to relieve Lady Strachey, who had hitherto been on constant call. The appointment of the widowed Mrs. Vicary Gibbs was to have the happiest consequences the following year, when she married the Queen's nephew, Andrew Elphinstone. The Princess celebrated her birthday quietly at Appleton, where the Court was in official mourning and in private grief for President Roosevelt. The silent rocket bombs falling in Windsor Great Park without any preliminary whistle of warning were no doubt the primary cause of the Appleton sojourn at this time of the year. Ten days later expectation of Germany's surrender recalled the King to London and the Princess returned to Windsor. Then suddenly the war in Europe was over.

Princess Margaret flung her German books on the floor and announced that she would learn the wretched language no more. The King faced a blaze of arc-lights as he made a film of a speech he was to broadcast. The speech was not immediately made, nor the film shown until the Powers could agree on their public announcement of victory. There occurred a day of hiatus and indecision, although people were already gathering outside the Palace and cheering and singing.

And then the great balcony windows were opened and

the King and Queen and the Princesses were recalled again and again. "We went out eight times altogether during the afternoon and evening . . . a great reception." All London —like all the Allied world—was delirious with excitement and rejoicing. For the Princesses the evening brought an Arabian nights adventure when, squired by two Guards officers, they went out among the crowds incognito. Squeezed in the great jostle of humanity, they, too, called "We want the King! We want the Queen!" until the royal couple came out again. Later on, during that night of excitement, the Princesses went down the Mall to Whitehall, ducking—still unrecognized—under the chains of linked hands made by the revellers. "It was absolutely wonderful," Princess Margaret wrote to a friend. "Everybody was knocking everybody else's hats off, so we knocked off a few, too. Everyone was absolutely marvellous. . . ." More quietly the King recorded this outing in his diary, and added, "Poor darlings, they have never had any fun yet."

The next two jubilant days saw the Princesses sharing in the State Drives through bedraggled streets where bunting could not camouflage the bomb scars, but helped to hide the lack of paint. On both nights balcony appearances were necessary to acknowledge the great crowds at the Palace gates. On May 13th, Princess Elizabeth and her sister went to the National Service of Thanksgiving at St. Paul's, and this was followed by a journey to Edinburgh to take part in a similar service in St. Giles' Cathedral. Next day, after all-night train travel, the Princesses attended the King and Queen in the Great Hall of Westminster, when the Lord Chancellor and the Speaker presented addresses of congratulation from both Houses of Parliament. A minor side-effect of the public enthusiasm was the appearance of sackloads of mail addressed to Princess Elizabeth and the appointment of a third lady-in-waiting, Lady Egerton, to help cope with it.

In June the Princess went to Wales to inspect 3,000 Girl Guides who had gathered from all parts of the Principality, and a similar ceremony occurred in July when she paid a brief three-day visit to Northern Ireland with her parents. It seemed appropriate that she should change once more into a uniform emblematic of her girlhood. On V.E. Day (for Victory-Europe) she had appeared on the Palace balcony in the khaki of A.T.S. uniform. On V.J. Day (for Victory in Japan), August 15th, peace, after six years, once more reigned over the entire world, and she again appeared and reappeared on the balcony with the King and Queen and Princess Margaret. But this time she wore a girlish summer frock, a symbol of youthful demobilization that caught the jubilant fancy of the public.

From homely domestic incidents to State pageantry of the most historic character, the events that befell Princess Elizabeth in the first year of peace rippled outward to ever-wider horizons of experience. The Balmoral holiday itself had a new and unfettered quality and the evening talk was "of nothing but stalking and antlers and points." On September 3rd, with the anniversary of the outbreak of war sealed at last in finality, the King decided to enjoy all the sport that Balmoral could provide and, wearing a pair of her father's plus-four trousers, the Princess went off with Margaret Elphinstone and soon shot a stag, a fact engraved on a silver table-mat that henceforth always stood beneath the King's plate. George VI noticed with pride that she shared his love of sport and keen proficiency with rifle and rod.

In contrast, that autumn the Princess sponsored her first godchild, the infant son of King Peter and Queen Alexandra of Yugoslavia, at his christening in a chapel of Westminster Abbey. No sooner was the baby Prince in her arms than he commenced to kick and wriggle so much that, as the fond mother, Queen Alexandra, noted, "Poor Lilibet looked completely scared. But she never faltered. . . ." King George VI had been King Peter's godfather, so here again the ceremony bore an intrinsic pattern of continuity, though in little more than a month Peter was to hear his country proclaimed a republic by the Communists.

Meanwhile the girl who had seemed scared to hold a squirming baby resumed the duties that already fitted her like a glove: taking the salute at the graduation parade at Sandhurst, reviewing the Army Cadet Force in Hyde Park, watching a parade of Canadian airwomen and so forth. Through long years of unwavering tradition the graduates of royalty have been trained in a smooth progression from the small events to the large, first from small ceremonials at a parochial level to initiate the fledgling, progressing stage by stage to the discharge of the most important national functions.

By March, 1946, the month before her twentieth birthday, Princess Elizabeth was sufficiently versed and nerved to undertake a first major public ceremony on her own, a three-day visit to Northern Ireland. This was to embrace the full honours of State and would include the launching of the aircraft carrier, H.M.S. *Eagle*. The Princess sailed from Greenock in the new cruiser *Superb*, her own banner of arms at the masthead, the destroyers *Fame* and *Hotspur* in escort. It was, of course, the first time her standard had flown at sea, her first voyage in her own right in a warship, and her first solo journey outside the mainland.

There was a gale warning, but the Princess actually enjoyed a smooth crossing. Her speech at the Belfast shipyard of Harland & Wolff blended praise of the British shipbuilding industry, of the Fleet Air Arm, and of the emotional quality of British naval tradition, "something so very much our own." The following two days were devoted to a systematic and busy tour of the counties of Tyrone, Fermanagh, and Armagh. In a Belfast linen store the Princess exclaimed with genuine pleasure on being presented with a pair of monogrammed sheets and asked to see the person who had done the fine embroidery. She was taken up the stairs to the workshop, there to meet an elderly widow named Eliza Regan. "Your poor eyes must ache," said the Princess impulsively, a phrase remembered and repeated in Belfast long after the photographs of greater events had been put aside.

Thus, already, the Princess was garnishing the grand occasions with her own personal sincerity and compassionate insight. These are endearing attributes, and the Press soon served to make them widely known. Now, too, in that springtime of 1946, the Princess could return to London and tease Lieutenant Prince Philip by telling him of her own naval experience, her own life at sea. The rest of 1946 included the great victory parade through London, the initiation of the Princess as a Bard of Wales, and scores of public ceremonies and events. But behind the public pattern of life the return of Prince Philip was above all to enrich the Princess's life with vital new significance as she approached her coming-of-age.

When Princess Elizabeth first met Philip of Greece and Denmark in July, 1939, at Dartmouth, she knew nothing about him other than that he was the nephew of her "Uncle Dickie" (Lord Louis Mountbatten) and was decidedly the most handsome and endearing young man she had ever met. Before Prince Philip received his first naval assignment to the battleship *Ramillies* at Colombo, they met again and they exchanged Christmas cards the following year. They were both great-great-grandchildren of Queen Victoria. Princess Elizabeth could also boast of a dash of Danish blood from her great-grandmother, Queen Alexandra, just as Prince Philip could from his grandfather, Queen Alexandra's brother, that Prince William of Denmark who had become King of the Hellenes by invitation. The Christmas cards led to an exchange of letters and King George VI's diaries show that Prince Philip spent a leave at Windsor in mid-October, 1941, when he entertained the King with a light-hearted account of his adventures in the Mediterranean.

The next two years fostered the friendship of sailor Prince and Windsor Princess, as we have seen. She soon learned about his boyhood at Kensington Palace as well as his schooling at Cheam and Gordonstoun, and his unhappy family background of parental separation. With her ever-active curiosity, the Princess must have admired his knowledge of the world, knowledge that ranged from the Indian Ocean to the lagoons of Venice, from the swimming-pools of Alexandria and Cairo to the tip of Southend Pier. Prince Philip saw the Windsor pantomime, *Aladdin*,

in 1943, shortly before his appointment as first lieutenant
to the destroyer *Whelp*. Laughing immoderately from the
front or rushing behind the scenes to give advice during
the intermissions, he enhanced the Princess's own excitement and enjoyment in the performance. For the next
two years, while naval service took him from Algiers to
Tokyo Bay, their relationship was reduced to the delays
of a war-time correspondence. As all the world now knows,
the photograph of the Prince, clean-shaven in naval uniform, appeared on the Princess's dressing-table, and was
cautiously replaced in due course by a more discreet like-
ness showing the Prince all but hidden behind a furious
nautical beard. Then, early in 1946, Princess Elizabeth
shyly told Bobo and other confidantes, "Someone is coming
tonight!"

With Princess Margaret, dinner for three was served in
Princess Elizabeth's crowded, somewhat cluttered sitting-
room. The subject of their talk was inevitably romantic,
for they were shortly to meet again at the wedding of Mrs.
Vicary Gibbs to Andrew Elphinstone, and the ensuing reception at the Savoy Hotel. Princess Elizabeth was one of
the bridesmaids, and thus when the first engagement rumours spread some months later a photograph of them
together, Prince and Princess, was to prove a boon and a
blessing to newspaper editors, the Princess in a diadem of
rosebuds and lily-of-the-valley, the good-looking young
naval officer standing at her side.

Suddenly, as the observant Miss Crawford noticed, "Lilibet began to take more trouble with her appearance . . . it
seemed to matter more to her what she wore at this evening party or that. Then I would find that Philip had been
there!" The musical show *Oklahoma* was the theatre hit

early that summer and the song "People Will Say We're in Love" seemed to haunt the young couple whenever they went dancing. As early as September, 1945, an article in the Athens royalist newspaper *Hellenicon Aema* rumoured an engagement and caused the hard-pressed Buckingham Palace secretariat to issue a denial. A feverish reaction from war news and battle headlines now made the public follow every fragment of news concerning the Princess with a mixture of romantic wishing and affectionate guesswork. It was news, for example, when the Prince and Princess went to the London Hippodrome to see Ivor Novello's *Perchance to Dream,* though they were merely two guests in a party of sixteen.

On four separate occasions through 1946 and into 1947 Princess Elizabeth's engagement was rumoured in print and four times denied by the Palace. It was the word "engaged" that enabled these denials to be precise though misleading. Sharing a Balmoral holiday in 1946, Princess Elizabeth and Prince Philip could reach, if not a betrothal announcement, at least an implicit understanding. "Beside some well-loved loch, the white clouds sailing overhead and a curlew crying just out of sight. . . ." That was how the Princess herself described the scene. Still, nothing could be said, no betrothal hinted, no announcement released. The King could not believe that his daughter had fallen in love with the first eligible young man she had ever met. Nor would he have been sufficiently parental if he had not questioned the quality of Prince Philip's ambitions.

His cousin, Queen Alexandra of Yugoslavia, has explained how the Prince had to face "an appalling obstacle race of formality." First was his deep-rooted and long-

standing wish to become a British citizen. Having earlier
been advised to wait until the Greek monarchy was restored, he now found himself asked to delay again, lest a
slur on the Greek royalist cause should arise if one of the
family renounced his nationality so soon after the new
King had returned to the throne. Then too there were
questions of the young man's rank and civil status. Taking
his father's name, Prince Philip properly came from the
old Danish royal house of Oldenburgh. The nearest English equivalent of "Oldcastle" seemed to have undue Fal-
staffian connotations. "Mountbatten" could be persuasively
argued as the equivalent of his mother's maiden name.
As for precedents, Princess Helena Victoria and Princess Marie-Louise, Queen Victoria's granddaughters, had
dropped their father's "Schleswig-Holstein" from their
names and yet retained the style of Highness. At this point
Prince Philip at once impressed and pleased the King, and
also banished the suggestion of ambition, by saying mod-
estly yet with determination that he would prefer to be
plain "Lieutenant Philip . . . , R.N."

Nursing her own secret wishes, Princess Elizabeth had
to endure an anguish of impatience as all these difficulties
were assessed. Scheduled ahead was the tour to South
Africa with the King and Queen, when for four months
she would not even see Prince Philip. Time seemed all too
short for so much discussion. Once in a factory crowd,
when engagement rumours were rife, some people thought-
lessly shouted "Where's Philip?" unaware that the cry
would cause her to return to the Palace on the point of
tears. Sensitive, impressionable, the Princess could not
help but recall the tragic story of Princess Charlotte, who
also had once been Heiress Presumptive. In her twenty-

first birthday speech, at all events, there occurred the
phrase "I declare before you all that my whole life,
whether it be long or short, shall be devoted to your
service." There seems a haunting dissonance in such a
phrase in such a speech on an occasion of celebration. The
speech was in preparation as the year 1946 drew to its close,
and there is a story that after Princess Elizabeth first read
the draft manuscript she returned it to the secretary, saying, "It made me cry."

The Princess was quiet and subdued as the preparations
for the South African tour neared completion. She was
apt to wait at the telephone for Prince Philip's call from
Corsham every evening and South Africa was much, much
farther away.

CHAPTER V

THE SAILOR'S BRIDE

THE PROPOSAL that the King should visit South Africa after the war had been suggested by General Smuts as early as 1943 and was tabled on the royal agenda with the formal approval of the British Government in March, 1946. The King's uneasy concern that he might be shirking his share of the post-war austerity and privations of his people in Britain was emphatically countered by Prime Minister Attlee's advice that any curtailment "would magnify unduly the extent of the difficulties we are facing."

Though fretting at the prospect of the long separation from Prince Philip, Princess Elizabeth had to accept her father's advice that she should wait before announcing any engagement. Meanwhile she collected her wardrobe for the tour without the intense enthusiasm that might have been expected after years of clothes rationing. For even the Royal Family was "down to the lowest ebb," the King had said, in discussing the clothing situation with Mr. Attlee.

On February 1st the royal party sailed on the battleship

Vanguard, which Princess Elizabeth had launched some two years earlier. The Princesses' cabins forward had been prepared with considerable ingenuity and decked with rosebud chintz, but a battleship is not the most comfortable craft, and Elizabeth's calm crossing to Northern Ireland had not prepared her for the heavy seas of the Bay of Biscay. "I for one would willingly have died," she wrote. "I was so miserable. . . . Everything hurtled about so much . . . it was exhausting trying to keep one's feet. . . ." But on the third day the seas abated, games were soon organized on deck and one or two of the officers were "real smashers." As the ship steamed southward through the sunshine only the news from home daunted the spirits of the royal travellers. The hardest winter experienced in the British Isles for sixty-six years had to be endured in the teeth of a coal shortage that caused constant fuel cuts, and the food rations were still little above subsistence level. ". . . we feel (I say we, but I really mean I) guilty to be away from it all," the Princess wrote on February 15th, two sunny days before the *Vanguard* arrived at Cape Town.

In the next two months, at the heels of their parents, the two Princesses were to experience all the kaleidoscopic wonders—and all the physical rigours—of a royal tour of the post-war modern pattern. Cheered always to the echo, welcomed everywhere superbly, they were fed such large meals after the lean years of war that the Queen had to ask for smaller menus, and they were rushed through a sustained schedule over thousands of miles that finally left them thin and worn out. The hospitality and generosity shown them could not have been more lavish. On March 3rd, Princess Elizabeth broke away from her parents' programme to open a new dry dock and found herself grasp-

ing a gift-box filled with diamonds. In Kimberley the De
Beers Company presented the sisters with two large blue-
white diamonds of the highest quality. In Southern Rhodesia the people subscribed to a birthday cheque of
£10,000. In Cape Town another casket of diamonds
greeted Princess Elizabeth's coming-of-age. And the Princess, for her part, discovered a country of unimaginable
greatness: Table Mountain, the Drakensberg and Victoria
Falls were like punctuation marks in the crowded pages of
the African scene.

This was the first time in history that a Royal Family
had ever undertaken such a tour together. For the first
time, also, Princess Elizabeth freely experienced the swift
new interest of flying, in a bush-hopping trip to the Free
State Game Reserve and then on a longer flight from
Johannesburg to Rhodesia. It was perhaps a convention
that the two Princesses should don white dustcoats and
head-scarves and ride on the footplate of their ivory-and-
gold "White Train," with its fourteen coaches, the longest
and heaviest train that had ever run on the South African
railways. Learning as much as she could beforehand of the
Union of South Africa, steeped during her Eton studies in
its racial and political history, the Princess Elizabeth had
anticipated the duality of a nation with two capitals, two
flags, two national anthems, two separated groups of cheering crowds, one white, one of darker skin. Less envisaged,
in all probability, were the swirling dust-clouds that en-
veloped the royal party at the native meeting-grounds, the
fresh beaches of the Indian Ocean, the barbecues with
open wood fires, the sight of thousands of tethered native
horses, the immense gathering of some seventy thousand
Basuto tribesmen, the salute of the hooded cobras at Port

Elizabeth, the incredible depths of the Crown goldmine, the alternative views of grandeur and glimpses of squalor.

To the native mind it was significant when at the hilltop of Cecil Rhodes's grave, the Queen Consort was unable to walk in high heels, and Princess Elizabeth took off her sandals to give to her mother and walked symbolically barefoot on African soil. Inspecting Basuto Girl Guides, the sister Princesses sympathetically visited a closed bus of Guides who were victims of leprosy. This royal gesture against superstition was widely praised. Arriving at Stellenbosch, the deliberate silence of the onlookers reminded the royal party that opposition to the idea of monarchy was still a political tenet of many South Africans, but the natural charm of the Princesses melted even republican hearts and the atmosphere noticeably softened. That evening King George made the splendid gesture of returning the Family Bible of President Paul Kruger which had been removed to London after the Boer War.

On Princess Elizabeth's twenty-first birthday it seemed fitting that the Heiress Presumptive should celebrate her coming-of-age not in London but in South Africa itself as a climax of the tour. In the morning, accompanied by Field-Marshal Smuts, Her Royal Highness inspected a great parade of the South African Army and took the salute. In the afternoon she saw a huge rally of youth organizations. In the early evening, speaking from a room in Government House, the Princess made her memorable birthday broadcast to five hundred million of her father's subjects. "I am six thousand miles from the country where I was born," she said, "but I am certainly not six thousand miles from home."

Her solemn act of dedication, her promise to devote her

"Here comes the bambino!" said Queen Mary. Princess Elizabeth of York, aged 11 months

Marcus Adams

Marcus Adams

H.R.H. Princess Elizabeth

Marcus Adams

The first picture at the Palace: The Princess Elizabeth, King George VI and his Consort, and Princess Margaret, 1937

Second Subaltern Elizabeth Windsor changes a wheel

Left: Bride and Bridegroom: the wedding picture that charmed the world. *Right*: The Crowned Queen at Westminster Abbey, June 2, 1953

The Times

Elizabeth II and her Commonwealth Premiers

Visitors at the White House, 1957

The Queen and Princess Margaret drive in the Irish State Coach to the Opening of Parliament, London, 1956

"Your Majesty, Chicago is yours!" The Queen and Mayor Dick Daley

Press Information Bureau, Government of India

The Crescendo welcome of India, 1961

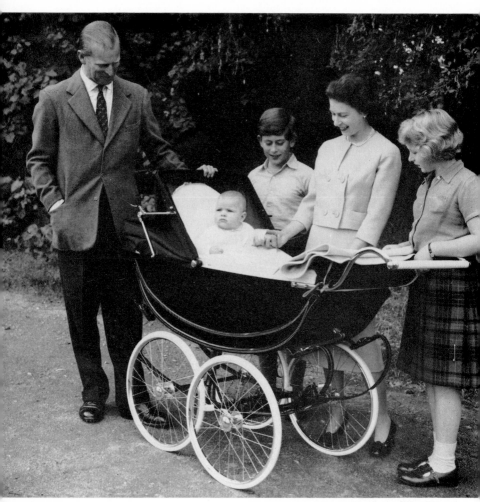

The Times

The Royal Family at Balmoral. Left to right: Prince Philip, Prince Andrew, the Prince of Wales, the Queen, Princess Anne

whole life to the service of the Great Imperial Family, the patent sincerity of her clear young voice, has outshone the memory of her central theme:

"But in our time we may say that the British Empire has saved the world first and has now to save herself after the battle is won. . . . It is for us who have grown up in these years of danger and glory to see that it is accomplished in the long years of peace that we all hope stretch ahead.

"If we all go forward together with an unwavering faith, a high courage and a quiet heart, we shall be able to make of this ancient Commonwealth which we all love so dearly an even grander thing—more free, more prosperous, more happy and a more powerful influence for good. . . ."

Returning on May 11th to the land of her birth, Princess Elizabeth danced a little jig of joy on the *Vanguard*'s deck. She returned to a wider, still more vigorous public life, driving with her parents to the Guildhall and then, a month later, repeating the drive in her own right to receive the freedom of the City of London. The British Commonwealth, she said on this occasion, was not so much a single act of statecraft as a miracle of faith. On June 12th, the King's official birthday, Princess Elizabeth rode at his side for the ceremony of Trooping the Colour in the role that had become traditional for the Prince of Wales. The sight of her slim young person, mounted side-saddle and impeccably uniformed as Colonel-in-Chief of the Grenadier Guards, had a galvanic impact on the British public, who had, of course, never seen the Queen Consort in uniform and had not suspected that her daughter could be such a representative military yet womanly figure on parade. All the more intense grew the speculation on her engagement and the certainty that an announcement could not long be withheld.

Even in South Africa a provincial councillor had begged Princess Elizabeth to hint whether the rumours were true. The fever of curiosity was world-wide and imperative. Lieutenant Philip Mountbatten, as Prince Philip had become by naturalization, motored up and down between his naval training establishment in Wiltshire and Buckingham Palace during the early weeks of summer, but the clue lay with a widowed and reticent Princess who had quietly taken up residence with her Mountbatten sister in Kensington Palace, that same Princess who had lunched at Windsor Castle on the very day Princess Elizabeth was born.

Princess Elizabeth had already met Philip's mother, Princess Alice of Greece, and accepted and disregarded the physical handicaps that Princess Alice had conquered with courage and pertinacity akin to Helen Keller. A loving relationship was immediately established. Princess Alice wished to make a special gesture to show her own warm approval of her future new daughter-in-law, and this took the form of redesigning a treasured ring of her own, with a square-cut diamond, that had been given her by her husband, Prince Andrew of Greece. This was to be Princess Elizabeth's engagement ring. But when it was first slipped on her young finger it proved to be too large so, after a few days, it had to be returned and modified.

"Something is going to happen at last," Princess Elizabeth told a confidante on July 8th. "He is coming to-night." At midnight, the long-desired announcement was released, "It is with the greatest pleasure that The King and Queen announce the betrothal of their dearly beloved daughter, The Princess Elizabeth, to Lieutenant Philip Mountbatten, R.N., son of the late Prince Andrew of Greece and Princess Andrew (Princess Alice of Battenberg), to which union The King has gladly given his consent."

In her journal eighty-year-old Queen Mary noted, "I must say the young couple look very happy. I trust all will be well. . . . They both came to see me after luncheon looking radiant." Fortunately, a royal garden party was being held at the Palace the following day so the couple immediately appeared together in public. All the guests quite evidently wished to show their fond approval, but could find no convenient opportunity until the Royal Family crossed to their private marquee for tea—then at last an inhibited croak arose. Scotland enjoyed a more vociferous opportunity when the Royal Family took up residence at Holyrood House two weeks later and the engaged couple appeared at a Hamilton Park horse race. It was charming to see that the handsome Lieutenant Mountbatten bent over Princess Elizabeth, but not too attentively, and that they laughed a great deal together and talked like conspirators. As another auspicious touch the Princess's programme included the acceptance of the freedom of the city of Edinburgh. "I am glad that at a time of great happiness I should find myself in Scotland," she said, "for to me Scotland and happiness have always been closely interwoven."

It perhaps astonished Princess Elizabeth that after all the months of delay and discussion there still remained points of perplexity that her elders had overlooked. The surname that her children might bear became a matter of public surmise, for example, and the Archbishop of Canterbury had to draw the King's attention to the fact that Prince Philip was still technically a member of the Greek Orthodox Church.

The months of betrothal were busy. The wedding in Westminster Abbey was fixed for November 20th and Norman Hartnell did not hear until mid-August that one of his designs had been approved for the wedding dress. He had planned to interpret the motifs of the embroidery in fine white crystals and pearls, but after roaming the London art galleries for inspiration he utilised ten thousand costume pearls in a magnificent display of garlands of white York roses entwined with ears of corn, a sparkling motif repeated in a milky way of blossoms strewn on the fifteen yards of bridal train.

Two years after the war the absurdities of patriotism still ran strong. At one stage Mr. Hartnell was alarmed lest the satin of the dress should prove to be from silk spun by Italian or possibly Japanese worms, and was relieved, after telephoning the Scottish mill, to be assured that they were "Chinese worms—from Nationalist China, of course." Elaborate precautions had to be taken to ensure that the details of the bridal gown should not become known in advance, so inquisitive was the world Press.

The problem of Prince Philip's rank and title gravely exercised the King. To Queen Mary, an expert in precedence, the King explained that he was giving the Garter to the Princess on November 11th to ensure her seniority to Philip, who would be given it eight days later. He was also to be created a Royal Highness and ennobled as Baron Greenwich, Earl of Merioneth and Duke of Edinburgh. "It is a great deal to give a man all at once," the King wrote, "but I know Philip understands his new responsibilities." Even so, though conferred as a "Royal Highness," the Duke of Edinburgh was not created a Prince until Elizabeth, as Queen, corrected the anomaly in 1957.

The gremlins of austerity threatened the festivities. Even the use of rationed timber for the few wooden stands was tightly contested. The London District Trades Union Council passed a resolution, "The use of large quantities of scaffolding, timber . . . in view of the serious housing shortage would be unwarranted. We therefore urge the Government to prevent any dislocation of labour and materials by regarding this wedding purely as the domestic concern of the persons involved." At the War Office, it is said, the Quartermaster-General's department gloomily planned a khaki processional turn-out.

Then a happier plan prevailed—a Captain's Escort of Household Cavalry in full dress for the bride and bridegroom and a Sovereign's Escort for the King and Queen. In October the country's mood changed with an impulsive gust of romantic affection. "Slowly the King's advisers are realizing that Britain desires to rejoice aloud," wrote one spokesman, and Mr. Winston Churchill voiced the sentiment of the nation when he said, "Millions will welcome this joyous event as a flash of colour on the hard road we have to travel." Stores that had arranged to open on the wedding morning suddenly announced that their employees would be given a holiday.

On the wedding day itself their less fortunate sisters played truant in their tens of thousands, craning to catch a glimpse of the happy pair, the carriages, the foreign royalties. Five Kings and Queens attended the wedding, not all of them still in possession of their thrones, but it mattered more that the people of Britain attended in spirit, or as close as the barriers and soldiers permitted, thronging the streets for two days beforehand, while millions of stay-at-homes were no less loyally delighted that they could listen to the wedding service in their homes by radio.

At an ever-increasing tempo the wedding gifts poured into St. James's Palace, where Boy Scouts helped with the unpacking and arrangement. There were personal gifts, such as the picnic set from Princess Margaret and the wastepaper-basket from Bobo. There were presentations at an official level such as the grand piano from the R.A.F. and the thirty-piece dressing-table set, in silver gilt, from the heads of the Diplomatic Missions in London. But there were also hundreds of wedding presents of a more informal nature: a pair of evening shoes from displaced Latvians, a Shetland shawl from a group in a mining town, hand-woven rugs from a group of Brownies in Eire. There were gifts lavished with an eye to commercial publicity and gifts fashioned in tiny homes as labours of love. There were more presents than one imagined the Princess could comprehend, and yet she looked at them all and read every letter, though sometimes "touched almost to tears." As Miss Crawford said, "I think it was the first time she realized how many people loved her who had never seen her."

The King recorded that the bride looked "calm and composed." Old Princess Marie-Louise thought of her as "radiant and beautiful . . . no fairy Princess could have been more lovely." Queen Alexandra of Yugoslavia noted, "Lilibet looked pale but very lovely . . . utterly lovely." Perhaps there is always agreement about a bride. General Smuts of South Africa found his impression "beautiful but sad . . . sad, because she is serious and wise beyond her

years." The Archbishop of Canterbury emphasized in his
address that the marriage rite in Westminster Abbey was
"in all essentials exactly the same as it would be for any
cottager who might be married this afternoon in some
small country church in a remote village." To each his
view.

Mrs. Germaine Miles, one of the three Hartnell ladies
who helped to dress the bride, found her "so pale and
solemn that we were almost alarmed." Yet there seemed
reason for both pallor and alarm, because Princess Elizabeth was confronted on her wedding morning with almost
every bridal crisis that could occur. As her mother's sun-
ray tiara was being set upon the bride's head, the frame
broke and a jeweller had to rush it away by car to his workshop for hurried repair. The Princess decided to wear
the two strings of pearls that her parents had given her as
a wedding gift, but these were at St. James's Palace and the
secretary sent to fetch them unaccountably failed to return. (As a matter of fact, he managed to get through the
crowds, but found it difficult to convince the detectives of
his identity, and precious minutes elapsed before he completed his mission.) Not least, the bridal bouquet could
not be found, though it was at length traced from the
porter's lodge to a cupboard where a footman had placed
it to cool. But finally all these crises were overcome and
the ten-minute wait allowed for emergencies gave the
Princess a chance to move to the window. "For a long
time," says Mrs. Miles, "she studied the people and then
gave a little smile."

In Westminster Abbey itself, for those with an eye to
omens, the bride's train momentarily caught on the altar
steps and the King and Lord Milford-Haven helped to

free it. This train gave trouble again at the start of the
return procession and Princess Margaret stepped forward
to help the two young kilted pages, Prince William of
Gloucester and Prince Michael of Kent. Princess Elizabeth
had also evidently intended to place her bridal bouquet
on the tomb of the Unknown Warrior, as her mother had
done before her, but for once a premeditated plan succumbed to emotion and the bouquet was taken back to
the Abbey the following day.

Yet as one of the guests put it, "A young English girl
was married in the family church . . . you forgot the trap-
pings, the plumed helmets, the jewelled Orders." The
bride herself chose to heighten this simplicity by selecting
a special descant for the Scottish metrical version of the
Twenty-third Psalm. She elected to promise to love,
honour, and obey. "*I Elizabeth Alexandra Mary, take thee,
Philip, to my wedded husband. . . .*" She went to her wedding as seriously, as humbly and reverently, as in the mood
of her birthday dedication earlier in the year. . . .

The first week of the honeymoon was to be spent at
Broadlands, Earl Mountbatten's home. The bridal couple
left Buckingham Palace to drive in an open landau
through the November fog—the bride snugly ensconced
in a nest of hot-water bottles—and people gathered to
watch the honeymoon train along every mile of railway
track from Waterloo to Winchester.

But public interest could not be switched off nor the
newly wed couple permitted complete retirement. The
pale pink walls, the blue bathroom, the Salvador Dali
drawings, the flower-patterned chintz of the honeymoon
suite had to be detailed in print. The Romsey police had
to be augmented to keep watch on photographers who

crept toward the house through the bracken. When the young couple went to Sunday morning service at Romsey Abbey, sightseers carried chairs, ladders and even a sideboard into the churchyard, and a wild scramble over graves and tombstones occurred the instant the honeymooners reappeared.

Finally, the Princess and her husband put their heads together to devise a suitable message of thanks before seeking a less restricted honeymoon in the early winter snow and solitude of Birkhall. The message was deft and full of fun: "Before we leave for Scotland tonight we want to say the reception given us on our wedding-day and the loving interest shown by our fellow countrymen and well-wishers in all parts of the world have left an impression which will never grow faint. We can find no words to express what we feel, but we can at least offer our grateful thanks to the millions who have given us this unforgettable send-off in our married life."

The problem of a separate home for the new married couple seemed initially fraught with difficulties. So was the fulfilment of nearly every wish in those "horrid years," as Princess Elizabeth privately called them, of bleak and desperate recovery from the war. Early in her engagement the Princess had inspected with the King the rambling old mansion of Sunninghill Park. The royal househunters found the dilapidated rooms ravaged by years of rough Service usage, the main roof damaged by fire, the former trout lake choked by debris, and the weed-grown grounds littered by Nissen huts, some of which were occupied by squatters. The Windsor rural council had been offered this forlorn property for rehousing the bombed homeless and had declined it. Nevertheless the Commissioners of Crown Lands advised that a wing could be renovated with due economy in labour and materials and the work was started. Then within a month the Royal Family at Balmoral heard that the house had been gutted by fire.

Rumours of malicious arson became widespread, but the Berkshire police, on the evidence, ruled out the suggestion. "I can't believe it. People are always so kind to us," the Princess wrote. The flames had consumed her hopes of turning the house into another Royal Lodge, though her husband at least felt a sense of relief. The disappointment was to prove a blessing in disguise. Instead, the Duke of Edinburgh and his wife leased Windlesham Moor, which, with three reception rooms and five bedrooms, was as modern, comfortable, and secluded as could be wished.

Meanwhile, in London, the Duke had no more than a bedroom and bathroom adjoining the Princess's sitting-room in Buckingham Palace. There was a public wish that the Princess should have an official establishment removed from that of the King. (Indeed, this was so manifest that the young people compliantly made their town headquarters for a time in the Athlone suite in Kensington Palace.)

"When I die, Lilibet, you will have Marlborough House," said Queen Mary, with her acute memories of the era when that grand pile had been the home of the heir to the Throne. Gently the Princess reassured her grandmother that nobody wanted her to die for a very long time and a London house was needed much sooner than that. The happy solution, finally, lay in the successful rehabilitation of a royal white elephant. After using Clarence House as war-time offices, the Red Cross and St. John organization had just vacated this former home of the Duke of Connaught. In 1947 the house still lacked electricity and possessed not a single bathroom—although an antiquated bath was fitted in a cupboard—and a stout heart was needed to find one's way through the warren of dark panelled corridors to the few scarred and derelict rooms with surviving Nash ceilings and chimneypieces.

Since Parliament voted only £55,000 for the modernization, much of this sum being for the provision of electricity, central heating and the modernization of the kitchens, service quarters and Household offices, the residue of the final cost may have been quietly disbursed from private royal funds. Fifty-five workmen were engaged for a year and Princess Elizabeth took great pride in watching the house emerge from its squalor to a new and contemporary beauty.

Her wedding gifts included many pieces of furniture of the latter half of the eighteenth century to give the rooms a pleasing stylistic unity. The Hepplewhite mahogany breakfront bookcase and writing desk, the combined gifts by subscription of many members of the Royal Family, became notable features of her sitting-room. Here, too, were card tables of Georgian walnut and a chest of drawers in satinwood, the burnished brown and pale gold of the woods playing counterpoint to a Chinese needlework screen in turquoise, golden yellows, and coral. Actually English-made in Cambridge, this was the gift of Queen Mary, together with an Adam-style sideboard and four serving-tables which could have been made for the dining-room, matching within inches the frames of plaster moulding on the walls. Here the Princess so vividly imagined paintwork of a delicate Adam green that she eventually mixed the paints herself to get it precisely right.

The final task of assembly was a joy. A dignified yet homely setting for a grandfather clock of the William and Mary period was discovered in an arched recess off the main corridor. The perfect setting for a satinwood veneered commode was found in the drawing-room, its pale amber emphasized by the paler upholstery of the modern arm-chairs. With the main pieces disposed, the Princess turned to the precise placing of the smaller but no less valued gifts: clocks and mirrors, lamps and vases. The Georgian portraits in the dining-room, which had always hung there through living memory, were perfect. The new Halliday portraits of herself and her husband graced the sitting-room, and elsewhere contemporary pictures, with emphasis on landscapes and seascapes, supplied a light and fresh atmosphere. A collection of original modern cartoons and caricatures by Bateman, Lancaster, Giles and others occupied one of the corridors. Many of these referred to royal incidents and reflected the outlook of the new occupants, for it has been aptly said that one cannot imagine the Duke of Clarence hanging the latest lampoons of Gillray or Cruikshank about the house.

Those interested in Queen Elizabeth II's first married home can, in fact, find it described and pictured in detail in Christopher Hussey's book *Clarence House,* from the massed array of family photographs on the Princess's desk to the electric pastry oven in the basement kitchen. In 1948 it seemed natural and indeed inevitable to Elizabeth that she should share her enjoyment in the assemblage of her home with the people whom, she knew, gave such love and thought to her. This sacrifice of privacy via the camera met with warm and immediate appreciation: not least, in the words of one spokesman, as "a sign of modern royalty's new approach to the people."

The same freshness of approach was apparent when the Princess enlisted the members of her new Household. The selection of Lieutenant General Sir Frederick Browning as her Comptroller and Treasurer was highly popular. The Princess was not surrounding herself with "grey-beards in satin breeches." Sir Frederick's war-time reputation as the creator and commander of Britain's first paratroop force, whom he had headed so heroically at Arnhem, commended him to the public imagination. Again, the Princess's new private secretary, Major Martin Charteris, had the equally romantic aura of a young man —he was then in his thirties—who had served with Intelligence in the Middle East and had survived a series of adventures in the desert only to be torpedoed in mid-Atlantic where, "with faultless manners," it was said, "he apologized to his fellow castaways on a raft for being seasick."

With Lieutenant Michael Parker, the Duke of Edinburgh's private secretary—who first met his future employer as his opposite number on an escort destroyer in the North Sea—these were vigorous contemporary figures. Evolving new working systems to match their new responsibilities, they sat at unaccustomed desks in the eighteenth-century atmosphere of the Household wing in Ambassador Court, while Clarence House received the plaster and paint of its fresh new façade.

While the fifty-five artisans hammered and painted in Clarence House—which was not, in fact, ready for family occupation until July, 1949—the Princess and her husband lived mainly at Buckingham Palace and spent their free weekends at Windlesham Moor. Their staff recall their laughter and happiness: they might be found scampering gleefully along a corridor or dancing together to the radio, and a large sofa which had stood isolated in the window of their sitting-room was now drawn snugly up to the fire. When the Duke began working at the Admiralty, he left home promptly every morning like any other young husband and, as evening drew on, the Princess would watch from a Palace window like any other young wife, craning for the first glimpse of his tall, striding figure.

One of the early public engagements they shared together was a visit to the London docks to inspect the sailing ship *Pamir*, then training New Zealand officers and men. "I would like nothing better than to make a trip in sail when I go to sea again," Prince Philip chanced to say, and journalists seized, with an air of surprise, the hint that he planned to return to sea. But this prospect was one the Princess took completely for granted. Her former governess had given her some well-meaning advice: "You must not expect the honeymoon to last forever. Sooner or later you will meet the stresses and strains of everyday life. You must not expect your husband to be constantly at your side. . . . A man has his own men friends, hobbies and interests. . . ." Crawfie was now married herself and settled in Scotland, but the Princess had listened attentively and the counsel lingered. In 1948 the Princess and the Duke could visualize years stretching amply ahead for both their joint and separate "professional" careers. It was as if they were twin barques, now sailing apart, now side by side, seldom diverging and always borne on the same strong currents of purpose. "I can, I know, always count on you, and now Philip, to help us in our work," the King summed it up, in a letter to his elder daughter which she always treasured.

The King was indeed convinced that the Princess, though so young, was already equipped to take the helm of the ship of State, at least in a limited sense. He had precisely this in mind in March, 1948, when he announced that, with the Queen and Princess Margaret, he proposed to visit Australia and New Zealand the following year. It could be foreseen that Princess Elizabeth and presumably the Duke of Edinburgh would then act as Counsellors of State with the Duke of Gloucester and the Princess Royal, but the major role of leadership in the public limelight would clearly devolve on the Heiress Presumptive.

It was also the King's happy inspiration that Princess Elizabeth should be invested with the insignia of a Lady of the Most Noble Order of the Garter on St. George's Day, April 23rd, two days after her twenty-second birthday and three days before the celebration of his own silver wedding. The day was further to be marked as the six hundredth anniversary of the founding of the Order, endowing Princess Elizabeth's investment, and that of her husband, with special significance. The full pageantry of the Order had not been seen at Windsor for nearly fifty years. The King revived it brilliantly, prescribing the wearing of the crimson velvet mantles with cordons and collars and hat, and the attendance of Heralds, Pursuivants, and Kings of Arms in their rich habiliments. The bestowal of the Order had reverted to the gift of the Sovereign only two years before, and to the acclaiming crowds it was a welcome splendour to see the King and his Queen and twenty-two knights walking in procession through the sunlight to St. George's Chapel. Here linked with the idea of Christian chivalry was the essential pomp and gorgeous colour of royal pageantry, the sense of history and tradition that forms one of the strongest bulwarks of the British monarchy.

Satisfied with his experiment, King George VI wished the meeting of the Order to be held annually. His illness intervened the following year, but whenever possible our present Queen has followed her father's wish, and the pageantry of the Garter—a reminder of the position of the Sovereign as the fount of honour—has become one of the rich and glowing enhancements of her reign.

Moreover, the festivities of her parents' Silver Wedding were scarcely over when, in the middle of May, the Princess Elizabeth and the Duke of Edinburgh undertook their first State mission abroad by paying a visit to Paris. Ostensibly this was to open an exhibition of "Eight Centuries of British Life in Paris," where, among other whimsical exhibits, Her Royal Highness was asked to admire her great-grandfather's top hat, preserved under glass. Yet there was nothing glazed about the fervour of the French welcome. As one Parisian said, "It was the day of liberation all over again," and the Princess divined that the spirit of freedom was being freshly welcomed as well as herself and she was so aware of what the French people had suffered that as she drove down the Champs-Elysées her eyes brimmed with tears. Overwrought by such a reception, she felt faint during the wreath-laying ceremony at the Arc de Triomphe and had to summon all her resolve and determination not to disappoint the crowds. Prince Philip was solicitous. Next day he also suffered from a touch of the jaundice that was liable to affect him when under emotional strain, and the Princess experienced something of the anxiety of any wife with a sick husband in a strange land.

Both nevertheless summoned up their resources, like actors going on to a stage, and went through the programme their Parisian hosts had laid down: church in the morning, the races at Longchamps in the afternoon, dinner at the Tour d'Argent and a short visit to a smart nightspot in the Rue Pierre Charron. These extramural Sunday activities caused a Scottish Sabbatarian to fulminate about "a dark day in our history." It seems more worthy of record that the French authorities issued a statement, "We in Paris loved Princess Elizabeth because she became *tout à fait Parisienne.*" The French knew nothing of Prince Philip's indisposition, but all Paris was firmly convinced that they knew all about the Princess. They were right, of course. Until then, the young couple had thought it their own secret that their married happiness was to be enhanced by a baby.

CHAPTER VI

WIFE AND MOTHER

THE ANNOUNCEMENT of Princess Elizabeth's happy antic-ipations was curiously timed. Issued from Buckingham Palace on the eve of Derby Day, it stated briefly, "Her Royal Highness The Princess Elizabeth, Duchess of Edinburgh, will undertake no public engagements after the end of June." The immediate result was a public demonstration of affection around the Princess's car at Epsom, the massing of an applauding multitude so firm and rooted that the police had to ride their horses into action to clear the way. The Princess did not refrain from joining the royal party in the usual walk to the paddock down the course. The cheers were thunderous, the crowds unwieldy and the cheerful, admiring cry of "Good old Liz!" characterized the day.

A current theory circulated that the announcement had been timed to protect the Princess from her unremitting sense of duty. The aftermath of Paris saw her visiting Coventry, Oxford, and Cardiff, besides the host of regimental inspections, prize presentations *et cetera,* and she had continued to accept a series of dinner invitations in Downing Street and elsewhere in order to acquaint herself more intimately with the background atmosphere of government life. Privately at home Princess Elizabeth got out the old high-slung pram that had not been used since Princess Margaret's babyhood and wheeled it along the Palace corridors, getting her hand in, as she explained. The coming event caused her no disquiet. "It's what we're made for," she shrugged, to an inquiring friend.

Meanwhile, the Princess saw her husband become a Freeman of the City of London and she attended the Royal Gallery of the House of Lords when he formally took his seat as a peer. At Windlesham Moor, during the pleasant waiting weekends, Princess Margaret had to beg her not to run with the dogs and showed sisterly solicitude with cushions and footrests. An avalanche of gifts began, including a ton and a half of diapers from America, which caused hilarity. A room at the Palace became a sort of packing-house where layettes could be prepared for other mothers. Because of her old dislike of knitting, Princess Elizabeth did not herself make any baby garments, but she accepted an offer by the Linen and Woollen Drapers Institution, of which she was patron, for a layette of fifty-five garments to be prepared by the twenty-five retired dressmakers in their Cottage Homes.

With her mother she agreed that the Palace schoolroom should be restored as a nursery, as in her own infancy. Her old cot and basket were brought out and renewed, not in blue or pink, but with silk of buttercup yellow. "Then no one can guess whether we want a boy or a girl," the Princess explained.

Yet this was not the only conspiracy of secrecy in the

Palace as the summer days gave way to autumn. While the Princess received her own doctors—Mr. William Gilliatt, Mr. John Peel, Mr. Vernon Hall, and Sir John Weir, she knew little if anything of the constant stream of specialists who now also called on her father. The serious vascular obstruction affecting the King's legs had been discovered. There was grave fear that his right leg might have to be amputated. The Palace preparations for the King's tour of Australia were secretly suspended, but the King insisted that no word of his condition should reach his daughter. The Princess's baby was born on November 14th and the King stopped hiding his own condition on November 16th.

Four days before her accouchement the Princess paid one of her usual private visits to Sir Alexander Korda's private cinema, this time to see a Burgess Meredith film. Two days beforehand, the serene wife and anxious young husband went out to dinner with Lord and Lady Brabourne at Earl Mountbatten's house in Chester Street. Cameramen were now patrolling the Palace entrances but a traditional clue of the immediacy of coming events was no longer available. The King had discovered that the attendance of a Minister of the Crown at a birth in the Royal Family was not laid down by statute nor could it be properly claimed as a constitutional necessity. After consulting the Government, the Private Secretary issued an announcement, "It is merely the survival of an archaic custom, and the King feels that it is unnecessary to continue further. . . ." After three centuries, the Home Secretary was therefore spared his usual wait.

But the people waited, drawn to the Palace as ever by the mystic compulsions of loyalty and the curious sense of participating in an event of true history. At eleven on

Sunday morning, the bystanders covered the steps of the Victoria Memorial as if awaiting a royal procession, and their vigil was maintained through the day. It was not until after 10 P.M. that a Palace footman walked across the courtyard with a message, and the tape machines of the world thrummed out the words, "The Princess Elizabeth Duchess of Edinburgh was safely delivered of a Prince at 9.14 P.M. today. Her Royal Highness and her son are both doing well."

Despite the late hour, eighty-one-year-old Queen Mary drove over from Marlborough House, "delighted," as she noted, "to be a great-grandmother." In the chilly November mist a police siren car had to beg the strange, singing throng on the pavements for quietness "as the Princess wishes to have some sleep," while in the Palace the staff toasted the health of the infant, "a lovely boy," all seven pounds, six ounces of him. In the morning the young mother may have been awake and happily gazing at her baby as the gunners of the Royal Horse Artillery in Hyde Park fired the forty-one-gun salute, a salute to the first child born in direct succession to the Throne for fifty-four years. Presently she confided her maternal sentiments to a friend in a letter, highly characteristic in its sweetness and simplicity, "Don't you think he is quite adorable? I still can't believe he is really mine, but perhaps that happens to new parents. Anyway, this particular boy's parents couldn't be more proud of him. It's wonderful to think, isn't it, that his arrival could give a bit of happiness to so many people, besides ourselves, at this time?"

The Duke of Edinburgh had dinner with his wife in her bedroom every night that week and gradually broke the news of her father's illness and the subsequent postponement of the King's planned Australian tour. King George could now take his doctors' advice and rest in bed, with the happy result that the risk of amputation disappeared. By December 15th, indeed, he was well enough to attend his grandson's christening. The last two of the names "Charles Philip Arthur George" were the King's, although Prince Philip's uncle, Prince George of Greece, also shared with the King the honours of sponsorship. The other godparents included Princess Margaret, the King of Norway, Lady Brabourne, the Hon. David Bowes-Lyon, and the baby's paternal great-grandmother, the Dowager Marchioness of Milford Haven. The Archbishop of Canterbury performed the ceremony, claiming jovially that he had never had a casualty at a christening. "Quiet as a mouse," the infant Prince indeed caused not a moment's concern. The King and Queen, Queen Mary, the Duchess of Kent, the Earl and Countess of Athlone, and some twenty-five others occupied the chairs in the gold and silver Music Room. Yet because Princess Elizabeth wanted a private and simple domestic christening for her son the guests also included Miss Willox, the Queen's dresser; the beloved Bobo and her sister, Ruby; the King's valet, and Mrs. Barnes, the cook from Windlesham Moor.

As 1949 opened soon after Christmas at Sandringham, Princess Elizabeth had the wry experience of an attack of measles that confined her to her room and separated her from her adorable baby. This touch of absurdity was nevertheless to usher in three years as complex yet simple, domestic, diverse and as tranquil yet troubled as any she experienced in her first thirty years of life. At the hub of her existence was the nursery or, rather, the nurseries in triplicate at Sandringham, Buckingham Palace, and Windlesham Moor, a domain the Princess shared amiably with the new nanny, Miss Helen Lightbody, until her wider duties drew her away. Then she followed the practice of her parents, laying down the régime, and visiting the nursery morning and evening, if not at other times, always charmed and delighted and overflowing with love for the wonderful baby boy that was hers.

Nor was the first flush of joy marred by anxiety for her father. After the King's 1948 operation, the family thought him to be on the way to complete recovery. When another operation seemed advisable the doctors presented their case with tact and the Princess could continue her public and private life with an easy heart.

A series of provincial grand tours began. They had been shrewdly planned originally to focus attention on the Princess's activities during her father's absence in Australia. The Princess and her husband busily visited Lancashire in March, Wales in April, and Northern Ireland in May, among other areas. In June the Princess took over the Trooping the Colour ceremony as her father's deputy, and this, too, was an event scheduled originally for his anticipated absence overseas. As things were, the King sat in an open carriage and watched his elder daughter with pride and satisfaction. Storm flies plagued her police horse, Winston, but she handled the golden chestnut with correct yet sympathetic *haut école* technique, giving him just sufficient rein and firmness. The King congratulated her.

The Princess was happier side-saddle on a fractious horse than she was to be in vicious seas on the battleship *Anson* that same month when visiting the Channel Isles. Prostrate with sea-sickness, her entourage doubted whether

she was fit to land on the isle of Sark, and General Browning went ashore to explain the situation to the welcoming
officials. A doctor was summoned, but when she realized
what was happening, the Princess roused herself. This
was the first time any member of the Royal Family had
ever visited little Sark officially. "Of course I'm going," she
said, in that familiar phrase. "I *won't* disappoint those poor
people." Again the motor torpedo-boat made its violent
passage through the squally sea. Now in the trough of a
wave, now on the crest, the Princess had to try three times
before stumbling on to the quay. Yet she made her tour of
the island, smiling, in a jolting horse carriage. She looked
"enchanting in a summery lemon dress," the Dame of
Sark recorded, and the islanders little knew what the effort
had cost the Princess.

On July 4th, 1949—"Independence Day," as the Duke
pointed out with a twinkle—Princess Elizabeth and her
husband moved into Clarence House. The Princess's personal banner was broken from the flagstaff; the sentries of
the Welsh Guards took up their ceremonious posts at the
gates and, incidentally, General Browning was struck by
the number of applications from Buckingham Palace
policemen who wished to transfer to the Princess's service. For their busy royal lady the move was at first more a
matter of "dropping one's things" than of residence. Official visits were paid to Dartmouth and Derby, Mansfield
and Nottingham, Shrewsbury and the West Riding of
Yorkshire.

Gossip at this time was occupied with the Duke's alleged
attempts to broaden his wife's horizons by introducing her
to his own friends, who were supposed to be old naval
cronies. Yet the Duke's tastes were essentially aristocratic;

the "Edinburghs" had now increasingly shared the same
social background for many years and their busy private
lives left little time for relaxation except with understanding relatives and intimates such as the Brabournes, the
Wernhers—Mrs. David Butter and Mrs. Harold Phillips
are both Wernher daughters—the Elphinstones and a few
others. Meeting Mrs. Roosevelt the Princess could ask
sober questions about women's detention houses and be
thought perhaps over-serious. With closer friends she could
steep herself in an atmosphere of family gaiety which
ranged from racing lore to witty reminiscence. But as the
summer of 1949 progressed the Princess seized every opportunity to be alone with her husband. An approaching
separation was again all too near.

The Duke had forcibly argued that he could not receive
naval promotion without earning it, and on October 12th,
he left for Malta as first lieutenant on the destroyer
Chequers. In November the Princess waited only for
Prince Charles's first birthday and the necessary events of
her engagement-book before flying out to join him for
Christmas.

Malta was a new experience. The vine-hung terraces of
the Villa Guardamangia, where Lord and Lady Mountbatten were her hosts, the sunshine on the lemon trees,
the red earth, the narrow streets with their old palaces
and churches, all were like painted stage scenery for her
role as a naval officer's wife. She needed merely to play at
being a Princess, touring the tiny local hospitals, admiring
the babies, flowers in her arms.

In the morning, waking to church bells and the cries and
clamour of the island, the Princess breakfasted and dealt
capably and quietly with her mail from London. Then

she was free to relax, perhaps for a casual anonymous drive with Countess Mountbatten, perhaps an expedition by launch to one of the neighboring creeks and bays. There were pleasant afternoons when she could sit and watch Prince Philip play polo, and evenings when they could dine and dance together at the local hotel. For the first time she could enjoy real privacy away from the atmosphere of Sandringham or Balmoral, where royal business was never quite forgotten.

On returning home, Princess Margaret proved perhaps the most enthusiastic listener to her adventures. The two sisters were flung closely together once more, during Prince Philip's absence, sharing public events as well as family intimacies. They went soberly to the House of Commons to hear one of the economic debates that followed the devaluation of the pound. They had earlier visited the Old Bailey to acquaint themselves with procedure and had heard part of a murder trial. With their parents, the two sisters shared the enjoyments of the "royal command" variety and film performances; and they were part of the royal company to inspect in the ballroom at Buckingham Palace the gallant crew of H.M.S. *Amethyst*, of Yangtse River fame. They motored from Sandringham to Newmarket to watch Captain Boyd-Rochfort's racing string at the gallops. They went to Aintree to watch the fortunes of Monaveen, Princess Elizabeth's steeplechaser, and had the satisfying excitement of seeing him take every fence and come in fifth when all but seven horses had fallen.

With Princess Margaret now almost twenty against her sister's age of twenty-three, the disparity of their years seemed at last to have lessened to nothing. Princess Margaret, with her pleasant chatter, was a pipeline to the parochial news of the Palace. The coming appointment of Group Captain Peter Townsend as Deputy Master of the Household and his hopes in piloting the flying entries in Princess Margaret's name in the King's Cup Race were no doubt discussed. A sympathetic listener, Princess Elizabeth also soon had her own special news, for a second baby was on the way and she ardently hoped that this time it would be a girl.

Flying to Malta in good time for her birthday, she could confide these tender prospects to her husband in an atmosphere of sunny warmth. If the island seemed remote from the economic blizzards and political deadlock at home, she might agree that she had earned a respite. Until the announcement on April 17th stating, "Her Royal Highness the Princess Elizabeth, Duchess of Edinburgh, will undertake no further public engagements," constant news coverage had told how consistently and conscientiously she had been doing her job, with visits to the new town of Crawley, to Bath and Bristol, with visits to airfields and exhibitions, military inspections and prize presentations, City luncheons and Guildhall dinners. The King found her a dependable mainstay during the State visit of President Auriol of France and Madame Auriol, both of whom grew familiar with the Clarence House nursery and its engaging eighteen-month-old occupant. "We became firm friends," said the President and later he was to report to his own voters, "If there have been clouds over the friendship which unites our two peoples, I can assure you nothing of them remains."

The *entente cordiale* was, in fact, conspicuous when the Princess flew home from Malta after another completely relaxed and enjoyable stay. Heavy thunderstorms blan-

keted the route to London and the pilot of her Viking
aircraft decided to return to Nice, where the Princess had
lunched. Equal to the occasion, the airport police chief
drove her into town in his black Citroen in which, as he
merrily explained, prisoners were sometimes driven to
jail. A suite at the Hotel Negresco was ready, and that
evening the British Consul-General took the Princess for
a drive along the Lower and Upper Corniche. Thus for the
first time the Princess saw the pleasure domes of Monte
Carlo and the headlands and inlets that had been so familiar to Prince Andrew, her father-in-law.

When she retired for the night the brilliant lights of the
Promenade des Anglais were dimmed and the traffic
diverted, a truly Gallic gesture so that she might sleep undisturbed.

Princess Anne was born at Clarence House on the sunny
Monday morning of August 15th, 1950. Again the crowds
loitered through the weekend at the approaches to the
Princess's home, first to be rewarded by a glimpse of Prince
Charles setting out for a drive with his under-nanny, and
a flurry of doctors at 10.30 and the arrival of the Queen
at a quarter to twelve.

On leave from Malta the Duke of Edinburgh immediately telephoned the King at Balmoral and then telephoned his grandmother and mother at Kensington Palace.
"It's the sweetest girl." The baby weighed six pounds.
Seven days later the Duke was at Balmoral, rabbiting over
Tulloch with the King, the Princess having insisted that
he should not waste his leave. Seven days more, and he
was back in London to register the birth of "Anne Elizabeth Alice Louise" and to receive her ration book and

identity card, still the necessary perquisites even of a Princess of the Welfare State five years after the Second World War. When Princess Elizabeth went to Scotland with her sturdy son and tiny daughter in mid-September, the Duke had returned to Malta to take up his command of the new frigate *Magpie*, but he flew back to London for the christening on October 21st. These minutiae of travel illustrate how the speed of flying and increasing informality of royal train travel were heightening the ease and freedom of royal movement.

Prince Philip's eldest sister, Princess Margarita of Hohenlohe-Langenburg, was also an important visitor as a godmother at the christening, sharing the responsibilities of sponsorship with the Queen, Princess Alice of Athlone, Earl Mountbatten of Burma, and the Hon. Andrew Elphinstone. Prince Philip's second sister, Princess Theodora of Baden, had already been entertained at Birkhall in the course of visits to her son who was at school at Gordonstoun. Now Princess Elizabeth began to welcome her sisters-in-law at Clarence House, and with them a happy coming and going of nephews and nieces. Even the youngest of Prince Philip's sisters, Princess Sophie of Hanover, was twelve years Princess Elizabeth's senior, and yet by a second marriage she had a son who was only a year older than Prince Charles and a second son divided by only a month or two from Princess Anne.

All three sisters were able to entertain Princess Elizabeth with tales of her husband's childhood. There was the time when the sight of an Algerian carpet-seller had spurred young Philip to seize the family's best Persian rugs and attempt to hawk them in the streets. And at a royal funeral —to be exact, the somewhat gruesome reinterment of his grandparents some ten years after death—sheer nerves at his first heavy State occasion had caused him to be sick into a borrowed top hat. Princess Elizabeth could not hear enough of his earlier background and happily her natural curiosity was soon to be assuaged. King Paul and Queen Frederika had invited the young couple to Athens and the Princess's Christmas visit to Malta afforded a highly convenient opportunity. Princess Elizabeth had not expected to find Athens decorated and *en fête* since the visit was supposedly unofficial. Yet guns boomed as they entered Phaleron Bay and waving people lined the avenue of red-pepper trees to the capital. King Paul drove them himself in an open car and, after a short rest at the royal palace, they sped on to the summer palace twenty miles away at Tatoi for a family luncheon with Prince Philip's mother and Prince and Princess George of Greece. The next day saw a State drive through the streets to the City Hall, and once again the reception was fervent, with almost more Union Jacks waving than Greek national banners.

Prince Philip must have been delighted by the enthusiasm for his wife and himself in the land of his birth. For the Princess, too, here was another novel change of atmosphere from the calm of Clarence House to the clatter and clang of the Athens trams, the babel of motor-horns, the pellucid light on the old stucco palaces. With the King and Queen of Greece she climbed to the white vision of the Parthenon. The quarter of Kokkinia, though notorious for its Communist sympathies, was gay and smiling, and here the Princess was driven to the top of the Hill of Nymphs and introduced to the chapel of St. Elizabeth and St. Philip. The royal couple were told that the foundation-stone had been laid on their wedding-day and an ancient

Greek vase found on the site was presented to them as a keepsake.

Several days of ecstatic tourism followed. The Princess visited the Palace of Agamemnon at Mycenae, the ancient theatre at Epidavros, the white marble temple of Poseidon. The homeward journey through the Gulf of Corinth was broken at Delphi, and so Elizabeth of England walked the slopes of Parnassus and paid her tribute of admiration at the temple of Apollo.

The Duke of Edinburgh was in command of the *Magpie* until July 16th, 1951. The Princess remained in Malta until February 12th, and was there again for a month at Easter, this time taking in another expedition of discovery to Rome and Florence. The Villa Guardamangia was now leased in her name and the Clarence House staff shipped out plate and linen. There seemed no reason why Malta should not become a base for many a delightful stay, not in the immediate future—for the great tour of Canada was ahead—but in rosy indefinite prospect.

After the initial novelty Malta had quietly accepted her. The Princess could shop, a rare pleasure, sometimes without attracting a single spectator to her car. She could have her hair done in one of the cubicles of a salon in the Prince of Wales Road, reading a magazine under the drier like any other naval wife. Friends and relatives, among them Princess Margaret, flew out for a few days. There were picnics and drives, sailing and fishing expeditions, lazy chatty afternoons at the Marsa Club, days so healthful that a sleeping princess was seldom disturbed by the tocsin of church bells at 5 A.M.

Princess Elizabeth celebrated her twenty-fifth birthday in Rome. Here again the visit was private and yet the

personage and the person could not be separated. Her arrival with the Duke on April 11th was immediately marked
by a formal luncheon with President and Donna Einaudi
and Cabinet notabilities at the Quirinale Palace, but the
Italians sympathized with the desire of their guests to see
as much as possible of the glories of their country and
luncheon was followed by a tour of the Quirinale splen-
doura. The two-weeks' stay imposed no other official function. As Princess Margaret had done two years earlier, the
royal couple stayed at the British Embassy as the guests
of Sir Victor and Lady Mallet and were free to follow their
own devices. In the warm spring weather, the Princess
wandered in the Forum and visited the Capitol; she devoted a day to the Borghese Gallery, and paid a private
visit to Pope Pius. This too was linked with a thorough
exploration of St. Peter's, from the narrow walks within
Michelangelo's dome to the street of tombs of ancient
Rome only recently excavated in the foundations of the
basilica. The Princess's thirty minutes with the Pontiff
received Protestant criticism at home, but behind her were
the respectable precedents of visits by King Edward VII
and King George V. And was it wrong in any event to seek
some better understanding of the millions of Roman
Catholics who live beneath the British Crown?

At the weekend a visit was paid to Florence, by way of
Lake Bolsena and Siena, and even the Press cars tailing
the tourists were politely content to leave them to enjoy
undisturbed a roadside picnic. The young couple stayed
with Queen Helen of Rumania, Prince Philip's aunt, at
her villa on the slopes of Fiesole and, seizing the opportunity of visiting the Pitti Palace and the Uffizi, the
Princess was able to enjoy the paintings with little in-

terruption by cameramen and reporters. The Princess indeed achieved the considerable feat of engaging the respect
of the Italian Press. She pleased the Romans by going out
of her way to inspect the maternal welfare centres of which
they were proud, and great success similarly centred
around her visit to "Boys Town," the republic of street
waifs, where a boy of six recited a speech of welcome with
Latin gestures and presented a bouquet larger than himself. The Princess was on holiday and yet even on holiday
interested herself of her own free will in such social experi-
ments.

The volatile Italians showed their appreciation by not
shadowing her too intensively on her birthday, when the
Princess delighted them further by proving that her idea
of celebrating a birthday was a Roman holiday, driving
out to Tivoli to spend much of the day amid the gardens
and fountains of the Villa d'Este, lunching at a local
restaurant and spending the drowsy afternoon exploring
Hadrian's villa.

Princess Elizabeth returned from Malta to a crowded
engagement-book and a summer of maturing plans. Three
years earlier, in May, 1948, she had addressed the inaugural
meeting of the Council of the Festival of Britain 1951 in
these words, "I would suggest to you the importance of
setting the highest standards in everything you plan. This
lays a special duty on our craftsmen and manufacturers to
ensure that the design of all goods displayed in 1951 bears
the scrutiny of the world. The Festival of Britain 1951
may prove to be not simply an end in itself, but a beginning of many good things."

Now three hundred subcontractors had replaced the

slums on the south bank of the Thames with the Dome of Discovery and the Skylon, the Royal Festival Hall and architecturally varied pavilions testifying dramatically to Britain's resurgence. Nearly £12,000,000 had been spent in spreading the Festival spirit far and wide, and when the Princess and her husband walked round the Exhibition on the eve of opening day the phenomenon was virtually complete. A century had passed since the May day in 1851 when Queen Victoria and her consort had opened an exhibition of the best of their era, and now their great-great-grandchildren toured a commemorative display.

Early that summer the King, though tired, seemed to be recovering from his ills. He could pay official visits to Cambridge and the Midlands and felt equal to the State Visit of the King and Queen of Denmark. Striving to relieve her father of responsibility, Princess Elizabeth played her part at Clarence House by giving a buffet supper for King Frederik and Queen Ingrid with guests as diverse as Douglas Fairbanks, Jr. and Danny Kaye. Within the month, however, King George fell ill with influenza and the Princess had to deputize for her father throughout the State Visit of King Haakon of Norway. Amid the magnificence of the State Banquet at Buckingham Palace her great-uncle King Haakon listened to her speech of welcome with grave demeanour and twinkling eyes, thus softening the task of her initiation.

Coughing in his bedroom, the King needed no reassurance that his daughter had handled everything superbly. A day or two later, she again acted for him at the Trooping the Colour and the King watched by television. This was the occasion when the Princess appeared so dramatically in Guards scarlet as colonel-in-chief, yet the striking

effect was not unforeseen. The decision that the Princess
should take the salute was made some months beforehand
and the details were carefully planned, even to a semi-
rehearsal when the Princess, in her scarlet jacket and rid-
ing-skirt, mounted a dummy horse which had been bridled
and saddled in the King's study. George VI was concerned
with the correctness of the bearskin tricorne hat. To Aage
Thaarup, the milliner, he remarked that it was not at all
what he had expected. But he was satisfied.

Subsequently, while the King rested at Windsor, the
Princess's programme included visits to Worcester, Bir-
mingham, Norwich, Manchester and Portsmouth and activities as different as a jazz festival and the opening of
the Antique Dealers' Fair. On her train journeys and at
home she filled spare minutes with memoranda and books
dealing with the Dominion of Canada. The long-mooted
proposal that she and her husband should visit the Dominion had swollen from a scheme for ten days in three cities
to a coast-to-coast itinerary embracing cities, towns, vil-
lages, hospitals, regiments, pulp-mills, and parks, and a
journey by sea, land, and air of sixteen thousand miles.
The maps and plans for the trip could no longer be spread
comfortably on the Duke of Edinburgh's drawing-board
and eventually the Princess, her husband, and her secretary, Martin Charteris, had to finally approve the routes
with the Hon. Lester Pearson, Canadian Minister for Ex-
ternal Affairs, by crawling over a huge map unrolled on
the floor.

Major Charteris left at the end of July for the pilot
tour, which now also included a "side-trip" visit to the
United States. The Princess eagerly discussed the project
with every expert she could meet. Her wardrobe alone,

involving some thirty different ensembles, each to be approved in designer's sketch, modelled and twice fitted, necessitated a series of appointments which would have exhausted most women. "I will do whatever they want," said the Princess, as each government of each of the ten Canadian provinces enlarged its plans for receiving the representative of the Sovereign and indeed suggested a programme she could not have possibly carried out in the time allotted for the trip.

Then all these complex arrangements were jeopardized because the King had to undergo another operation. The gravity of his illness could not be minimized. Princess Elizabeth and her husband had been due to leave on the *Empress of France* on September 25th. This sailing was at first postponed and then cancelled at the request of the Canadian authorities. The King, however, progressed satisfactorily. And so the Princess and her husband left London in a B.O.A.C. airliner just after midnight on October 8th. The quiet farewell in the King's sickroom that night was a sad one for father and daughter. The Princess carried with her a sealed envelope to be opened in the event of the King's death and she knew that it contained her own draft Accession Declaration and a Message to both Houses of Parliament. This package alone burdened her mind with the deepest anxiety.

Princess Elizabeth landed with her husband at Dorval Airport, Montreal, and at first Canadian observers found her nervous and shy. She was, in fact, tired after a seventeen-hour flight as well as gravely concerned about the King. A crowd estimated at fifteen thousand had to watch her in awkward silence from a remote distance across the runway. Then too, in spite of the landing at Montreal, the tour officially started in the city of Quebec, where the royal tourists arrived by train. It received, too, the most exhaustive and exhausting Press and radio attention hitherto staged.

Canadian and American journalists and photographers sought to give exclusive coverage one step ahead of all rivals and, in addition to 125 correspondents accommodated on the royal train, no fewer than 4,500 applications were made for badges or passes to cover one phase or another of the trip. In Ottawa a reception for 400 correspondents appeared also to be attended by 600 of their relatives. Though the newspapers next day carried many interviews, the Princess largely had to confine herself to shaking hands. At one reception the Duke of Edinburgh angrily declared "This is a waste of time!" when he found himself shaking hands with correspondents who had already been presented, but the Princess rarely faltered.

At every stop there were government officials, mayors, municipal councillors and leaders of local organizations, all with their wives, waiting their turn in line. As Alex Faulkner of the *Daily Telegraph* summed up, "Undoubtedly too many lesser office-holders managed to take up precious time by insisting upon their right to be presented, and quite a number got presented by 'hedgehopping' from place to place." In Toronto, it is said, the Princess shook three thousand hands in a day. The Canadian Press itself began to urge that too many "brass hats" were seeking attention. But Prince Philip then pointed out in a speech that since he and his wife could not meet all the Canadian people, it was right and proper to meet their elected representatives.

Despite these undercurrents, the jubilant populace soon turned out en masse to greet the Princess. The tour that began so quietly developed by the fourth day into a fervent national jamboree. French Canadian Quebec was astonished that the Princess spoke French so perfectly. Some Ottawa spectators were moved to weeping when a goldenhaired little girl who had just presented a bouquet stood like a poignant symbol during the singing of "O Canada," with her head leaning against the Princess's side. One correspondent cabled an account of an Ottawa day that included thirteen functions, two speeches, an official luncheon and State dinner. "Thunderous cheers echoed from early morning until late at night. Throughout it all the Princess was smiling, gracious and apparently untired." Such a welcome, in fact, so invigorated her that she gaily joined in the square-dancing at Government House that night. The dance was impromptu. Bobo was sent out to buy the right skirt and blouse at a department store, and Prince Philip danced with a price tag still on his jeans. The Princess and her husband enjoyed themselves so much and danced so late that they had no time to change. To the delight of the crowds, they drove to the station still in their square-dancing rig.

The Princess liked to see the local newspapers night and morning, though the delirious "build-up," almost more lavish than she anticipated, soon rather troubled her. Conscious of the thousands who were penned in for hours awaiting the merest glimpse of her, she ordered her car to circle around stadiums twice whenever possible; and where the itinerary on sightseeing routes called for speeds of 25 miles per hour she ordered the cars slowed to 4 miles wherever people were gathered. Told of a delegation who had travelled hundreds of miles for a brief meeting—a story that cropped up all across Canada—she asked, "Cannot we give them extra time?" When a crippled boy failed to make his flashbulb camera work as she passed his hospital bed, she promised to return to him and, what was more, remembered to keep her promise. A large, deafening and unnecessary motorcycle escort partly hid her from the public, and she asked if it could not be diminished. These proofs of her thoughtfulness were not lost on Canadians. When Prince Philip conceived the idea of a plastic bubble over the car so that the Princess could be seen in bad weather, operatives in a Toronto airplane factory ungrudgingly worked round the clock to produce it.

At the outdoor civic reception in Toronto one observer noted that "thousands of people choked the streets as far as the eye could see," and the emotional warmth of the reception inspired Major Charteris to Churchillian heights as he repolished her speeches and attuned them more precisely to the audience. "Here the most spacious monarchy and the most powerful republic dwell side by side," the Princess found herself rehearsing, as she paid a tribute to Canadian-American relations. But then in her own words she spoke of her anxiety for her parents and what Canadian concern had meant to them. "We have been deeply moved by the knowledge of your love," she said, unable to reveal how deeply the repeated inquiries after her father's health had gripped at her emotions.

Talking to her mother every morning by transatlantic telephone, Princess Elizabeth heard with relief of the King's daily progress. Indeed, before she left Ontario, he was sufficiently recovered to sit in a chair and receive a few family visitors. This heartening news brought high spirits to the royal train chugging its whistle-stop way across the prairies. Prince Philip's valet had patronized a shop in Toronto devoted to practical jokes. So now fiendish sets of joke false teeth flourished at breakfast, rubber snakes leapt from tins of nuts, rolls of bread squealed when touched, a mock bell pusher gave an electric shock—and at every crowded level crossing the Princess and the Duke hurried out to the rear observation platform just as elated as the good folk who had come to see them.

The tour was, however, held late in the year and zero weather threatened the success of the Calgary rodeo. Squads worked all night to free the frozen arena and the Mayor warmly ensconced his guests in electric blankets. Flurries of snow hid the peaks of the Rockies as the train progressed toward the Pacific. It brought photogenic herds of elk to feed near the railway line. Yet even in the snow people still waited. At a little halt at ten o'clock one night even the royal staff were moved to find people waiting in a blizzard, with a band playing under the arc lights. This undeterred throng greeted the Princess by singing "It's the Loveliest Night of the Year."

The news correspondents were now inclined to lament the twelve- and thirteen-hour days imposed on the Princess in the East. Two correspondents on the Press train had dropped out from nervous strain. But at Vancouver the Princess was overjoyed to receive a letter from her father, and Major Charteris could reassure Western Canada, "The Princess is fit as a fiddle."

As the Duke of Edinburgh phrased it, "It's not how many thousand miles we've travelled. It's the people we've seen." To keep themselves alert in the stunning din of the crowds, to make it easier to watch the continual dizzy "long blur of people," the royal couple set themselves to spot the radio commentators. It ranked as a special triumph if a broadcaster was detected and induced to respond to a special wave or smile.

Devising such breakwaters against the unavoidable tedium, leading the Princess on the infrequent occasions when she seemed uncertain, the Duke was a tower of strength. On the other hand, in Vancouver the royal couple heard of an Indian princess who had, of course, "travelled a great distance to be presented." Prince Philip said with some asperity, "That Indian Princess stuff is out!" But Princess Elizabeth proved her womanly patience and the Indian princess was duly received. Then too there was the great "smiling controversy." People accustomed to the Princess's smiling photographs were disappointed, it seemed, if she did not beam constantly. Finally, however, it was agreed that she looked regal when grave and serious, and so all was well.

Fourteen days of hustle earned the couple a blessed three-day respite on Vancouver Island at Eaglecrest, a private lodge vacated for the royal visitors. For a day rain hissed past the windows, and they sat reading and writing. Yet as soon as the weather cleared they were out and about, exploring the estate and fishing on a murky sea. At this stage Pierre Berton, the Canadian writer, summed up their trip west saying, "The Princess had travelled close to ten thousand miles by aircraft, train, limousine and destroyer; inspected twenty-one guards of honour; signed twenty-one golden books. . . . She had eaten Nova Scotian and Laurentian trout, Cape Breton partridge and Winnipeg goldeye, elk, grouse, wild goose. . . . She had been given twenty-three official bouquets (almost all from little girls in gossamer dresses). . . ."

The return leg of the journey was to be even more arduous and exacting. In one day, leaving her Port Arthur hotel at 9 A.M., the Princess inspected lines of ex-Servicemen in snow and slush, toured the city by car, visited a grain elevator, repeated most of this programme in the neighbouring town of Fort William, and then flew to North Bay, where she met the seventeen-year-old Dionne quints. At 4.30 P.M. the royal couple then arrived at Montreal for another string of presentations, a drive through the city and a hockey game. Early the next morning 7,000 students of McGill University roared "Yea, Betty! Yea, Windsor! Yea, yea, Betty Windsor! Rah, rah, rah." And with this the royal tourists started seventy miles of processional drives, miles so blurred with human faces that photographers and dignitaries in the royal procession had to close their eyes to ward off dizziness. The Princess flinched only when she found she was expected to lunch in full view of a thousand people, many of whom were jockeying for position. Her staff quietly insisted on private arrangements.

There followed a visit to Montreal University and an aircraft factory, a City Hall reception and a vast civic dinner. Then as the Princess concluded her last event of the following day, a boulder of masonry crumbled from a flag-burdened plinth and hurtled down within a yard or two of the red carpet. It fell among shrubs, one might add, where the Princess could not possibly have been standing, although this was to be recounted one of the narrow escapes of her life.

After the uproar of Montreal, the two-day visit to Washington seemed at first like a rest cure. The police chieftains had not recovered from a Presidential assassination attempt the previous year, and the hundreds of policemen milling about at the airport and the extraordinary security precautions along the city route gave the visitors the impression that in this land of the free there were more police than people. President Truman quickly dispelled the illusion. "When I was a little boy, I read about a fairytale Princess—and here she is," he said charmingly in his speech of welcome. His cordiality was sincere, for he also wrote to the King, "We've just had a visit from a lovely young lady. . . . As one father to another, we can be very proud of our daughters. You have the better of me—because you have two!"

Blair House was similarly a homely and welcome corrective. The White House annex for special Presidential guests possessed the upholstered, restful flavour of being second cousin to No. 10 Downing Street. And gradually as the Princess "took in" the sights of Washington—visiting Mount Vernon, the Capitol, the Library of Congress, and the Supreme Court—the general American delight and enjoyment in her presence became manifest. At a reception given her by the Washington Press Corps, the Princess faced perhaps the toughest, most cynical and least vulnerable band of men and women in the world, and conquered them by her "composure, modesty, and her own expert professionalism." (It amused her later that her visit shared honours in *Life* magazine with a gangster's funeral.)

Then too her professionalism was measured once again by the remarkable reception given at the British Embassy for Congressmen and their wives, the U.S. Cabinet, the Supreme Court, the Diplomatic Corps, members of the

Press and others. In two hours, the Princess and the Duke shook hands with 1,600 guests, chatting with some and smiling on all, a prolonged and dizzy task completed to the concluding handshake for an aged Negro Embassy messenger, the final courtesy in thanking the bandleader for his music. A Washington columnist summed up America's opinion, "You heard no mutterings from cynics, chauvinists, professional proletarians. Royalty would not fit into this country's scheme of things, but how glad you are for the British that they have a Princess so capable."

Before leaving the U.S. the Princess had hoped to see the New York skyline from the air, but this plan was frustrated by bad weather. The official tour was resumed in Canada after a free weekend at a palatial summer cabin in the Laurentians and next swung through New Brunswick, Prince Edward Island, Nova Scotia, and Newfoundland. Looking back, in a farewell broadcast from St. John's, the Princess recalled "the towering buildings of your big cities . . . the charm of your smaller communities . . . the greater future I have seen in the eyes of hundreds and thousands of children."

But she could not begin to describe a thousand incidents, lit even in recollection by an excess of flash bulbs . . . the pleasant young mayor who grinned as he handed her a rolled typescript and said, "The speech, ma'am," the mayor in quest of novelty who insisted on singing a ballad of welcome. On the debit side, the Princess acknowledged the failure of her little joke about Niagara Falls, "It looks rather damp." Local patriots seemed so mortified that she quickly added, "But it's magnificent!"

The forces of nature brought the tour to a crescendo as the visitors left Portugal Cove, St. John's, in a tender which was swept end to end by heavy seas. Prince Philip succumbed but the Princess was unaffected, an immunity she mercifully retained through gales encountered by her liner *Empress of Scotland* going home.

Though the Princess had found Canada "a second home in every sense" she had not anticipated the praise so grandly voiced by Mr. Winston Churchill at the traditional welcome-home Guildhall banquet. "None has surpassed in brilliance and in living force the mission you have just discharged. The whole nation is grateful to you for what you have done and to Providence for having endowed you with the gifts and personality. . . ."

This widespread satisfaction delighted the King, who could now see the fruit of his own training. His daughter had given him proof of her ability at the very hour when his own powers seemed at their lowest ebb. Now, apart from a troublesome cough, he could feel his health returning. At the end of November he left Buckingham Palace for the first time since his illness, but before motoring down to Royal Lodge for a weekend, he sent a note to the Princess at Clarence House. "To mark the return . . . from your and Philip's most successful visit, I propose to have you both introduced into the Privy Council. In other words to make you both Privy Counsellors."

George VI had at last acknowledged that he would not be able to face the strain of the postponed tour to New Zealand and Australia, but he experienced a hopeful flush of well-being. In the New Year the Princess Elizabeth and her husband were to undertake the tour for him instead, while he could cruise on a quiet, private visit to South Africa in the spring sunshine.

❧❧❧

CHAPTER VII

QUEEN REGNANT

D URING CHRISTMAS at Sandringham in 1951, relaxed and
content with the children and the family, Princess
Elizabeth studied the itinerary of the proposed Australian
and New Zealand tour of 1952 and she may well have
echoed her father's cry on an earlier occasion, "It's aston-
ishing what they expect us to do!" But the Princess would
never spare herself if others failed to spare her. Sir Frederick Browning presented as the final programme a document of meticulous timings and subdivided columns, with
every detail accounted, but one date stood out signifi-
cantly. On February 7th the Princess was scheduled to
board the liner *Gothic* at Mombasa in Kenya for the eight
days of official engagements at Colombo in Ceylon. This
was to inaugurate the tour proper. A week in Kenya had
been made a prelude to the tour at the Princess's special
wish. The King had spoken so often of the vast country
and its wonderful possibilities. The Princess longed to see
the region in which her parents had spent such a happy
and exciting holiday in the early years of their marriage,

and she planned to make a film to show her father the landscapes and wild life that he remembered.

A day of joy occurred at Sandringham when the King chanced to put his walking-stick to his shoulder and remarked, "I believe I could shoot now." This was hailed as a token that he had taken a new grip on life. On New Year's Day the King went out shooting at Heath Farm. The Princess and her mother were so reassured that they played truant two weeks later to go to the races at Hurst Park. The next few days were spent with sturdy, three-year-old Prince Charles and little Princess Anne. The evening of January 30th saw the Princess at a happy theatre party with the King and Queen, the Duke of Edinburgh and Princess Margaret, at Drury Lane, celebrating both the King's recovery and a bon voyage. The musical show, *South Pacific*, with its songs of nostalgic distant islands, was the King's choice; the Royal Family were happy together and moved by the prolonged ovation of the Drury Lane audience. Princess Elizabeth and her husband were to leave London airport at noon the next day in the B.O.A.C. Argonaut, *Atalanta*, for an overnight flight to Nairobi, and the King came to see them off. The photograph of the tired and haggard monarch has been printed perhaps too often, and we have too seldom seen the happy picture of the Princess Elizabeth, framed in the doorway of the airliner, smiling and gaily waving farewell.

The aircraft touched down briefly for refuelling in the desert evening at El Adem in Libya. Next morning the Princess and the Duke arrived punctually at Nairobi, having travelled 4,400 miles. Within twenty-four minutes after leaving the plane the Princess visited her first African hospital. The maternity hospital was new and four hours earlier, had housed not a single patient. A selection of expectant and recuperating mothers and black babies, borrowed from other institutions, however, now filled every bed. In sharp contrast to the London chill, the Princess and the Duke received a theatrical first impression of Nairobi: the African women in their flamboyant headbands lining the streets, the exotic blooms, the vast colourful Afro-European crowd at a garden party where, as a reporter cabled home, "Fellows in leopard skins were eating cream buns next to women dressed for Ascot."

The next day the Princess fulfilled her ambition to visit the game reserve of the Nairobi National Park. Armed with her 16 mm. movie camera, she was particularly charmed by the small and shy dik-diks. This endeared her to game-wardens who were accustomed to people being interested only in lions. Actually the Princess had never seen an African lion. In the Nairobi reserve, however, she was able to film one with its kill ten yards from her bush wagon. "This has broken my luck," she said.

The following morning, the royal party—with Lady Pamela Mountbatten and Bobo, Major Charteris and Commander Parker, packed into cars for the ninety-mile drive upcountry to Sagana Lodge, Nyeri. The Lodge was a wedding present to the Princess and her husband from the people of Kenya. Welcomed by ten thousand natives as they passed through the market town of Karatina and coated in red dust long before the hunting lodge was reached, the royal couple were charmed with their gift. It was no more than a cedarwood bungalow reminiscent of the little house in the grounds of Royal Lodge, yet great thought had been devoted to its decoration and Princess Elizabeth knew that every stitch that had gone into its chintz curtains was a labour of love. From the windows one could gaze at the snow-capped peak of Mount Kenya, and the garden ran steeply down by zigzag paths to the Sagana River. The Lodge was intended to be the royal couple's home for five days before they flew to Mombasa to join the liner *Gothic*. Only Lady Pamela and Miss Macdonald shared the sleeping accommodation in the house (even Clarke, the detective, had to be accommodated with the others under canvas), and the Princess and the Duke rose at dawn to go riding. The stay was full of African alarums and excursions: a herd of elephants came near and the Princess dashed to take pictures, a wild elephant was loose in the night in the compound and the staff were on the alert in case marauding baboons should break into the bungalow and try to eat the new lampshades. This had already happened not far away, at the resthouse of Treetops, where the Princess was to spend the night of February 5th–6th, and indeed she decided not to attempt to raise her personal banner there in case a baboon should steal it.

The fame of Treetops, Mr. Sherbrooke Walker's hotel-in-a-tree, was world-wide, though it consisted of little more than a dining-room, three bedrooms, and an observation balcony built into the branches of a giant wild fig tree, thirty feet above the ground. On February 5th, the Princess spent the morning watching the Duke play polo eight miles away, and they arrived at the forest path leading to Treetops shortly before three o'clock. As soon as Her Royal Highness stepped from her car, she heard the trumpeting of angry elephants in the forest ahead and the sounds grew more awe-inspiring as the royal party made their way in single file—the Princess, the Duke, Lady Pamela Mountbatten, Commander Parker and Mr. Windley, the Provincial Commissioner—along the six hundred yard trail through the dense bush.

Watching for her from the observation platform, the hunter, Jim Corbett, has told how a herd of forty-seven elephants chanced to mass in the glade below him only a few minutes before the Princess was expected. Among them were three jealous bulls who began screaming with rage, and presently began circling round towards the path the visitors were to take. The noise was at its height and the elephants were crowded within ten yards of the foot of the ladder leading to Treetops when Princess Elizabeth appeared with her guide. A white pillowcase was fluttering as a danger signal; but a hurried consultation decided that the Princess should go on and, unhurried and undeterred, she made her way towards the elephants—and the ladder —over the open ground. A minute later the Princess was seated on the balcony and filming the elephants, which milled about below her for over an hour.

When tea-time came the Princess was still so absorbed that she asked if she could have a cup where she sat. In the clearing below her, two-thirds of it lake, the rest the hard-trodden ground of a salt-lick, she had seen a cow elephant suckle its young. A family of twelve baboons had come from the forest and one bold female climbed to the balcony to be rewarded with a sweet potato from Princess Elizabeth, who then promptly filmed her in close-up. Two male waterbuck raced from the forest in a desperate battle, ending their combat in a mêlée of splashing in the lake, where one mortally impaled the other with its horns and then defiantly trotted off. Five warthogs and a dainty doe bushbuck came to browse, and the Princess alternately used her movie camera and scribbled elaborate notes, often exclaiming how much her father would have enjoyed the scene.

As the shadows lengthened and the frogs became vocal, more animals than had ever been seen before at Treetops —as Corbett noted—emerged on the open ground. In the sunset, as the group talked in low voices, the Princess affectionately told Corbett of her father's shooting prowess. She knew precisely where he had been shooting at Sandringham that day and where he intended to shoot the next day.

At dinner a contretemps occurred when the kerosene lamp for the coffee was accidentally swept from the table and set fire to the straw matting on the floor. Frantic efforts were made to stamp out the blaze. Then the African steward calmly extinguished it with a wet cloth and the peril dissolved in laughter. Afterwards, from the balcony, the Princess could see nine rhino on the saltlick, half lit by a flood-lamp that simulated the moon, and she stayed there with her husband and her friends looking into the night.

In the morning the Princess was up at dawn, waiting with a light-meter until the first rays of the sun could give her a picture of two quarrelsome rhino in the clearing below. She was fresh, "with eyes sparkling," although she had spent so few hours in sleep.

The royal couple devoted the rest of the morning to fishing for trout in the ice-cold Sagana stream, and after an early lunch retired for a short siesta. At about half-past one local time, Major Charteris had just finished lunch at the Outspan Hotel across the valley. He was on the point of leaving for a visit of his own to Treetops, when he was summoned to the telephone booth. There he was confronted by a local reporter, who, white as chalk, said abruptly, "The King is dead."

The news had been carried in a Reuter newsagency flash to Nairobi, but no official message had come through, because the Governor of Kenya and his staff were all on the train for Mombasa. Major Charteris immediately told Commander Parker and tried to contact the deserted Government House. Nothing was said, for the tragic tidings were still unconfirmed, when the Queen strolled out to find Bobo and to say that she and the Duke would be riding earlier than usual next morning. At a radio set, Commander Parker failed to intercept any announcement, though the tone of the programmes suggested that his information was true. Nearly an hour passed before he went round to the wide window of the lodge and beckoned urgently to the Duke. His Royal Highness came out and was told what had happened, and then he went back gently and sadly and told his unsuspecting young wife that her father was dead and that she was Queen.

Major Charteris has said that she bore the shock bravely, "like a Queen." In a little while, she sat down to write messages to her mother and her sister, and to Queen Mary and the Duke of Gloucester. She called Bobo and asked whether mourning had been packed in her wardrobe. (Always carried against a Court contingency, it was with her luggage on the *Gothic*.) Then the Queen sat down again to write a series of telegrams to her various expectant hosts in the Dominions, regretting that her visit must be indefinitely postponed. While she was stifling the first shock of grief in these tasks at her desk, Major Charteris her private secretary asked by what name she wished to be known as Queen.

"Oh, my own name—what else?" she answered.

The question then arose whether it would be correct to sign her telegrams "Elizabeth R" (Regina) before the calling of the Accession Council. Major Charteris had translated a cipher telegram requesting her permission to call the first part of the Council, for her Proclamation, and the new Sovereign agreed that her queenly signature would be constitutionally correct. Pale but composed during this discussion, she presently could not trust herself to speak, and her husband led her away from the house and along the bank of the stream where they had fished so happily that morning.

Fortunately, the new Queen soon began the journey back to London. A Dakota aircraft was waiting at Nanyuki airfield, forty miles away, in anticipation of the Mombasa flight planned for the following morning. The Argonaut in which the Queen had flown out from London also happened to have landed at Mombasa and was now ordered to Entebbe, in Uganda, to await the royal passengers.

At five o'clock all was ready for departure from the lodge. But first the Queen summoned each member of the staff who had attended her, the cook and houseboy, the Askari officers and police and drivers, to give each of them a signed photograph and a gift. Her African chauffeur flung himself down to kiss her feet. All along the dusty roads to Nanyuki, Africans stood with bowed heads, offering their silent tribute of sympathy.

At the airfield, precisely on the Equator, the waiting contingent of local newspaper cameramen were asked not to take photographs. The Queen was still wearing a flowered frock with white hat and gloves, and the cameras were respectfully lowered. After presentations, the Queen briefly smiled and waved as she entered the plane. Then the Dakota took off into the darkened sky and those left behind knew that they had witnessed a moment of history.

There was very little conversation in the cabin of the aircraft on the five-hundred-mile flight to Entebbe. The sky was spangled with brilliant stars and bush fires gleamed below in crimson patches. The pilot received a forecast warning of thunderstorms; and presently a radio message from Mr. Winston Churchill, the Prime Minister, expressing sorrow and allegiance on behalf of the Cabinet, was delivered to the Queen, "The Cabinet in all things awaits Your Majesty's command." At Entebbe airport, the Queen was met by Sir Andrew Cohen, Governor of Uganda, and his wife. Then the anticipated thunderstorm broke with tropical violence. The departure of the Argonaut was delayed for three hours, and it was nearly midnight local time before the Queen walked across the wet runway for the take-off. Once aboard, the royal couple retired at once to their sleeping berths in the rear cabin. The early hours of February 7th saw a touchdown for refuelling at El Adem, a British protectorate in South Arabia. To those with the Queen the time seemed to drag.

Presently Her Majesty appeared in the black coat and dress that had been brought from the *Gothic* and in the late afternoon, as the aircraft landed at London, she could see the black-clad group of statesmen, drawn up awaiting her. The Duke of Gloucester, her uncle, first came aboard to receive her, and to kiss her cheek. Beside the plane, Mr. Churchill, Mr. Eden, Mr. Attlee, and Lord Woolton were next to acknowledge her, in that order, as Privy Counsel-

lors. As Lord Woolton recalled, "This symbolic scene . . .
the new young Queen coming, unattended, down the gangway from her plane—was one that will never be forgotten. . . . It was a period of deep emotion for everyone
—and most certainly for the Queen, and yet, having shaken
hands with each member of her Council, instead of going
to her waiting car, she went along and spoke to the air
crew—royal courtesy took precedence over private grief."

The Queen wore no veil and her face was still unveiled
to the people as she reached Clarence House at five o'clock.
There Queen Mary was waiting to pay homage. "Her old
Granny and subject," she said, "must be the first to kiss
her hand."

The following morning Queen Elizabeth held her first
Privy Council at St. James's Palace, walking quite alone
and unattended from the old Throne Room into the En-
trée Room where Privy Counsellors, dressed in mourning,
were awaiting her. All made her a deep obeisance. The
young Queen was twenty-five years and ten months old
and nearly all those present other than her husband were
at least twice her age. She was "very serious, but completely composed." Walking to the table she took up the
copy of her Declaration, which had been mounted on a
board, and read it "in a clear and controlled voice," as
Lord Woolton noted:

"Your Royal Highnesses, My Lords, Ladies and Gentlemen,

"On the sudden death of my dear father I am called to
fulfil the duties and responsibilities of Sovereignty. . . .

"My heart is too full for me to say more to you today
than that I shall always work, as my father did throughout
his reign, to uphold the constitutional Government and

to advance the happiness and prosperity of my peoples, spread as they are the world over.

"I know that in my resolve to follow his shining example of service and devotion, I shall be inspired by the loyalty and affection of those whose Queen I have been called to be, and by the counsel of their elected Parliaments. I pray that God will help me to discharge worthily this heavy task that has been laid upon me so early in my life."

Shortly afterwards, in her own room at Clarence House, the Queen watched her proclamation by taped television and heard the change in the royal title that had been agreed upon at the Commonwealth Conference three months earlier, proclaiming her Head of the Commonwealth. After lunch, leaving for Sandringham by car, she could note the remarkable token of respect for the late King shown by her people. Nearly every man was wearing a black tie, as if for his own brother.

At Sandringham the body of George VI had been left uncoffined on his divan bed, in case the Queen should wish to see him. The Queen thanked her mother but declined. Such was Her Majesty's clear understanding of the memories she wished to cherish and of the limits of her emotional control. . . .

The funeral of King George VI was held in the wan sunlight of February 15th, 1952, at St. George's Chapel, Windsor. In three days nearly a third of a million people had filed past the catafalque in Westminster Hall, and each evening bouquets of little flowers, forbidden by the police but surreptitiously carried in, strewed the grey carpet. The Queen paid a visit for a short time to stand unnoticed at a side door. The mourning tableau of State was so like the

sombre scene for King George V in her childhood that
past and present merged. At Windsor the cry "God Save
the Queen!" followed the committal. The choir sang the
anthem "God be in my heart and in my understanding,"
and the Queen made her last reverent curtsey. The epi-
logue was to be spoken three years later when, in pouring
London rain, the Queen unveiled the Mall memorial to
King George VI. "Much was asked of my father in personal
sacrifice and endeavour. He shirked no task, however difficult, and to the end he never faltered in his duty. . . ."

This, too, was to be her own watchword, as it still is
today. The continuous business of State had accompanied
the week of grim ritual: the reception and hospitality of
the Kings and Queens, Presidents and Princes, Commonwealth Prime Ministers and others who came to the funeral; the reception of a deputation from the House of
Commons. At three o'clock, one afternoon, the Queen
received the High Commissioners and other representatives of the Commonwealth countries. Fifteen minutes
later she received the representatives of foreign Heads of
State. All but submerged in the flood of condolences, the
desk work went on, as it was now to go on throughout
the Queen's life. On the day before her father's funeral the
Queen approved the appointment of a new judge in Hong
Kong and the reappointment of three members to the
court of the Bank of England.

Four days after the interment she had a series of meetings with Mr. Dean Acheson, M. Robert Schuman, and
Dr. Adenauer (formally in the presence of Mr. Anthony
Eden, her Foreign Secretary), and showed herself already
well acquainted with the problems that were to come before a Lisbon meeting of the Council of N.A.T.O. The

Prime Minister had made his first report on February 12th and now reported weekly. A letter on proceedings in the House reached her daily. A series of audiences began with her Ministers, as they came to Clarence House one after the other.

But with every minute of her time so closely charted, it was noticeable that the Queen omitted no single opportunity to give love and companionship to her stricken mother and to Princess Margaret. She is said to have quietly called on Queen Mary for a few minutes every other day and, late every afternoon, she drew calm inspiration and contentment from the nursery hour reserved for her children. In all this, her husband was a constant rock of strength. After their first brisk response to the emergency, both the Queen and the Duke felt as if "anaesthetized and living in a vacuum"; such at least was the impression made on King Peter of Yugoslavia when he lunched at Clarence House. The young couple had imagined that they might again enjoy the private tranquillity of Malta, at some time after the overseas tour, and now all was changed. They both turned to their desks as if to an opiate, yet this mood also was to be replaced by growing hope. The Queen could not help but be stimulated by the brisk wave of confidence that ran through the nation, rejoicing at the dawn of a new Elizabethan age.

In mid-March Her Majesty held her first investiture in the Ballroom at Buckingham Palace, with the Duke of Edinburgh at her side. Although there had been argument for postponing the investiture—founded on the New Year Honours List—during the three months of Court mourning, the Queen realized that until the fifty-one new knights received the accolade, they could not receive their titles and she decided against delay. Seven posthumous awards were also to be made to the next-of-kin of dead heroes, and the Queen elected to deal with these decorations first and receive the parents and widows in an ante-room. So it came about that the widow of Flight-Lieutenant Alan Quinton received the first award from the Queen, a George Cross for an airman who had given an air cadet the only parachute in a crashing aircraft. Later that day, promptly linking her reign with that of Queen Victoria, the Queen also invested Private William Speakman with the Victoria Cross won for the highest courage in Korea. In April the Queen ceremonially distributed the Maundy money at Westminster Abbey, and so performed her first public function outside the Palace walls.

On her twenty-sixth birthday at Windsor, she yielded her colonelcy of the Grenadier Guards precisely ten years after she had received it from her father, and only then, after two months, did she enjoy the first breathing space since the return from Kenya. In the privacy of Badminton, with the Duke and Duchess of Beaufort, she was able to watch the three-day Olympic Horse Trials, and so find that complete relaxation which horses had always offered her.

She enjoyed this respite so much and found it so recuperative that she whisked her mother away the following week on the pretext of looking at some horses at Beckhampton. The Queen was subsequently to find with dismay that her racing and sporting proclivities gained an undue share of attention. Far less publicity was apt to attach to her enjoyment and knowledge of paintings at Windsor Castle and Buckingham Palace, or to the books she read when she had the time. This was natural enough, since one was in public, the other private, but the fervour for a new Elizabethan age elicited some disagreement on its nature. As E. S. Turner has summarized, "All had their own idea of what the Court ought to be. Some wanted it to encourage art and letters, opera and music. . . . Some wanted the Queen to lay fewer foundation-stones and visit more colonies. . . . Others, again, wished (the Court) to discountenance blood sports or to show more respect for the Sabbath. Still others wanted to see the royal children sent to ordinary schools. A few thought it would be a gracious gesture to receive the Duchess of Windsor."

The Queen was gradually to acquire the art of compounding these differences, but meanwhile she quickly and clearly demonstrated her individual technique of sovereignty. Sir Alan Lascelles, who had been her father's Private Secretary since 1943, became both her servant and her mentor. To her father's teaching, the Queen now added the lessons of Sir Alan's craftsmanship and experience. As the Sovereign's prerogative over the Government includes the right to encourage and the right to warn, so the Private Secretary, as her chief adviser, had the right to encourage and to warn the Sovereign. In the thick of the hunt for the formula of the new Elizabethan era, the Queen contributed her own steadfastness, and perhaps the outcome was best epitomized by Sir John Smyth, then one of Her Majesty's most junior Ministers:

"Faults and failings are inherent in any human institution, but in the shortest possible time the Queen set her own seal upon her age—and her seal was an innocent goodness of heart and devotion to duty which only the intellectual anarchist and the publicity hound have sought to deride. The Throne was to be the symbol of all those simple and good things of the heart which ordinary people hold dear . . . they were latent in (the Queen's) every gesture and accent, in her actions and in her speeches. And they were a clear statement to the nation that the ordinary human virtues are worth upholding and would be upheld by the highest lady in the land."

The Queen and her family took up residence in Buckingham Palace on May 5th. The Queen preferred not to move into her father's study: this was taken over by Prince Philip, while the Queen eventually worked in the pleasant sitting-room that had been her mother's. However, for the time being the Queen and her husband temporarily occupied the Belgian Suite, where the few favourite pieces of furniture brought over from Clarence House looked awkwardly makeshift. Furnishings moved back and forth between the two residences and it was five months before the second-floor suite was in order. A bedroom fireplace, for example, was a gift from King George VI to his wife, and the Queen Mother naturally wished to install it in her new home at Clarence House.

The Queen wished all her wedding gifts to have an effective place, if not at the Palace, then at Windsor or Sandringham. Queen Mary came to inspect the proposed changes and discuss which of her own pieces she wished her granddaughter to have. The old Queen was growing frailer; illness had confined her to her bed throughout April and, foreseeing that she might not be there for the Coronation, she insisted that this was on no account to be postponed. Anxious to cheer her up the young Queen went smiling to greet her grandmother on her eighty-fifth birthday, and Queen Mary talked of Queen Victoria's Coronation robes which she felt could form a precedent for the new Queen Regnant.

Setting in motion a whole new programme of preparation, the first Coronation Council was held at Buckingham Palace on June 6th. With the end of Court mourning, the Queen lived in a busy whirl of secretaries, visitors, diplomats, politicians, architects, designers, and portraitists. Her time was sedulously organized. The Eisenhowers had come and gone, the Regent of Iraq came to tea, the Sultan of Brunei brought an array of gifts. The Queen went into brief formal residence at Holyrood House and then travelled to Devon for a "visit of recognition" to the farms and manors owned by the Duchy of Cornwall, where every tiny village turned out to cheer and wave.

In the space of five months Queen Elizabeth II carried out one hundred and forty engagements, and indeed an article suggested that Her Majesty's health and vitality should be protected from her hereditary sense of duty. Within two weeks this caution was proved to be justified when, just as the Queen stepped on to the dais in the Throne Room to commence an investiture, she was seized with a sharp attack of abdominal cramp. Princess Margaret was telephoned in her suite upstairs and asked to be ready to act as deputy. But with rigid self-discipline the Queen completed the programme and returned to her rooms before taking to her bed for the rest of the day. The indisposition, which was happily only a passing one, sharpened the demand of a Parliamentary spokesman who pleaded, "We should lighten her load by denying ourselves the pleasure of her frequent appearances at public functions." So was the criticism against Queen Victoria completely reversed for her ebullient great-great-grand-daughter.

It has been said that Queen Elizabeth "took to queen-ship as a duck to water." It amused her to see the first Windsor milk-bottles with the initials E.R. and she said she had not felt like a queen till then. She considered that royal profiles on postage stamps had sometimes made the chin or forehead slope unnaturally and took her time in critically deliberating with the Duke of Edinburgh the portraits from which a semi-profile was finally selected.

In the same spirit, when desiring Norman Hartnell to submit designs for her Coronation gown, she knew precisely what she wanted and instructed that it was to conform in line to her wedding dress and was to be in white satin. Ultimately Mr. Hartnell submitted nine designs, with samples of the intended floral emblems. All these, the Tudor Rose, the Thistle, the Shamrock and the Leek, were the subject of infinite research and patient toil, but the Queen was unwilling to wear a gown bearing emblems of Great Britain without the emblems of the Commonwealth countries. So the lotus of Ceylon and India, the protea of South Africa, the wattle of Australia, the specific fern of New Zealand, the wheat and jute of Pakistan, and so on, were worked into a floral garland for the triumphant, ninth final design.

Typically, the Queen elected to wear Queen Victoria's Parliamentary mantle of royal purple and ermine when she opened her first Parliament in November and, as she drove in State through the streets to Westminster, Queen Victoria's diadem graced her brow.

A camera shutter clicked at the precise moment on the

homeward journey when, relaxed and exhilarated after duty done, she was smiling gaily at some incident in the crowd. The resulting picture of the young and happy Queen was widely reproduced, and was indeed soon to hang in shops, restaurants, clubs and offices throughout the Commonwealth. This also marked her initial appearance as the central figure on the Palace balcony when for the first time Prince Charles, the Duke of Cornwall, rising four, was brought out to see the crowds with his two-year-old sister. Then characteristically, after these splendours, the Queen changed clothes and took the children off to the birthday party of two-year-old Viscount Lascelles in Orme Square, Bayswater.

The foremost royal events of Accession Year concluded with the State dinner given to the seven Commonwealth Prime Ministers and other delegates who were again visiting London for a Commonwealth conference. If it could be said that no reigning Queen had opened Parliament for seventy years, it was also noteworthy that no reigning Queen—and no Sovereign so young—had ever presided over a family so international and representative. For the blood royal the Queen was already substituting the life-blood of democracy; and for the Divine right of Kings, she was submitting a Divine right to serve. Her very duties as Head of the Commonwealth were primarily unwritten and many were largely to be left to her own devising.

For her first Christmas radio broadcast from Sandringham, the Queen spoke with unfeigned sincerity of the coming Coronation:

"Pray for me on that day . . . pray that God may give me wisdom and strength to carry out the solemn promises

that I shall be making, and that I may faithfully serve Him
and you, all the days of my life."

As the complex and manifold preparations for the
Coronation lumbered under way, cumbrous and massive
as the gold State Coach itself, the central authorities of the
"Establishment" made a great blunder. They decided that
no part of the ceremony should be televised. They believed
that television would not heighten the religious solemnity
of the occasion and that the cameras would increase the
strain upon the Queen. But the decision to exclude television aroused, as one commentator expressed it, "a volume
of public protest that surprised both the Court and Downing Street."

Nor was public opinion in any way mollified when Mr.
Churchill announced in the House a compromise decision
that cameras would televise the processions west of the
Abbey screen. It was left to the Queen herself to smooth
out the difficulty with the Archbishop of Canterbury, Dr.
Fisher. Just as her father had welcomed the broadcasting
and the filming of his Coronation, in order that his peoples
might share it so the young Queen foresaw that the TV
camera could give millions a fuller and more significant
sense of participation. In the end, as we know, television
phenomenally enhanced the impact of the ceremonial not
only upon the Queen's watching subjects but upon the
whole world. And the colour films similarly enhanced the
splendour and nobility of the spectacle to the mind's eye
a few days later.

The twenty men of the Committee had, of course,
sought to uphold the ritual and yet lessen the demands
made on the slim and girlish central figure, but the Queen

herself was alert to fend off every such relaxation. A suggestion arose that the processional route through the streets should be curtailed. The Queen rejected it and asked that the route be extended through Northumberland Avenue and the Embankment so that thousands of school children could see her go by. At the traditional Court of Claims various people were advancing their hereditary rights to take part in the Coronation, and the Lord of the Manor of Worksop failed to uphold his claim to present the Glove which historically protects the Queen's right hand while carrying the Sceptre. The Manor had become part of a limited company and the Committee of Privileges decided that the right could apply only to an individual. The Queen was thereupon advised that the omission of the Glove would shorten the ceremonies at least by a little, but here, too, was advice that she declined to accept. And since the ailing Lord Woolton was not strong enough to fulfil his traditional function as Lord President and carry the heavy Sword of State before the Queen, she decided that the presentation of the Glove was a duty pleasantly within his scope.

Again, the order of the presentation of the Bible in the ritual was changed, and for the first time, at the Queen's behest, the Moderator of the General Assembly of the Church of Scotland was brought into the ceremony to present the Bible jointly with the Archbishop of Canterbury. Through an ancient royal emblem, armills or bracelets had not featured in a Coronation since that of Edward VI in 1547. Now the member nations of the Commonwealth presented a pair of armills of pure gold and the Queen agreed to their inclusion in the Service text as, "symbols and pledges of that bond which unites you with your peoples."

Fortunately in the early phase of planning, time and Providence allowed the Queen to discuss some of the changes with her grandmother. Queen Mary vividly remembered three Coronations, including her own, but was destined not to see another. She died on March 24th, 1953, only ten weeks before the fourth ceremony, in which a place was prepared for her. However as the old Queen had requested, the date of the Coronation was not altered.

Many crises of a more minor character occurred, however, before the successful culmination. The firm of pharmacists which had supplied the anointing oil since the coronation of Queen Victoria was discovered to have gone out of business, and the only phial of the sacramental oil preserved in the Abbey precincts had been shattered during a bombing raid. Finally an elderly kinswoman of the pharmacists' family was traced, and found to have kept for sentiment's sake four ounces of the original base of the oil. Two ounces were consecrated anew for the Queen.

Another difficulty arose from the acute shortage of royal carriages and of coachmen to drive them. The Queen hoped that the street processions could be completely horsed but, in a mood of stringent economy five years earlier, more than half the coaches and carriages in the Royal Mews had been sold. As it turned out, Sir Alexander Korda had purchased a number for use on film sets and was able to loan five two-pair broughams and two open landaus, and the War Office was able to make good the remaining shortage of vehicles and horses. But the shortage of coachmen was harder to solve. Even though ten members of the Coaching Club came forward to serve the

Queen in borrowed royal livery, her Majesty's coachmen
are by tradition clean-shaven. Tact smoothed the difficulty
and some of the finest moustaches of the Coaching Club
were eagerly sacrificed.

Like a vast mosaic the infinite meshwork of high ceremonial was gradually pieced together. In the Palace ballroom and art gallery the ground plan of the nave and
theatre of the Abbey was marked out to measure with
wands and tapes so that the Queen might rehearse her
movements step by step. In the Abbey rehearsals the Duchess of Norfolk acted as stand-in for the Queen, but on May
21st the Queen was present to watch a rehearsal and with
it hear some of the new music she had requested. The following day she herself joined in rehearsing the difficult
passage of the descent from the Throne. Bobo, the Queen's
dresser, the indefatigable Miss Macdonald, chanced to be
in the Abbey that day to inspect the robing-rooms in the
new-built Annex and made a surprising discovery. The
gilded furnishings and rich carpets were in position. Everything was arranged . . . except that nobody had thought
of providing the Queen and her ladies with mirrors. Here
was an oversight indeed, and so many bureaucratic delays
ensued that a mirror manufacturer did not receive the
urgent order to make and supply sixteen full-length mirrors until three days before the Coronation.

One imagines that the Queen laughed when she heard
of the omission. And we can follow her only in imagination as she rode through the streets to her crowning on
June 2nd in all the rich panoply and straitened loneliness
of queenhood. Those who watched the Queen in the Abbey
speak of her air of being alone in the midst of the multitude, her rapt attention upon every movement of the

ritual, "the sense of spiritual exaltation that radiated from her was almost tangible," as one of her Heralds noted. When she took her seat in the ancient coronation chair of Edward I, her eyes cast one swift glance toward her young son in the Royal Gallery. The Crown was slowly settled upon her head and her hands later rose in a movement to steady it. Then, presently, wearing her Crown, carrying her Orb and Sceptre, she went out into the streets where the London rain lashed down upon the immense cheering multitude.

CHAPTER VIII

AROUND THE WORLD

A s THIS DAY draws to its close I know that my abiding
memory of it will be, not only the solemnity and
beauty of the ceremony, but the inspiration of your loyalty
and affection." So said Elizabeth II, broadcasting on
Coronation night. That night and for three nights following the Queen and the Duke of Edinburgh were called
and recalled to the Palace balcony in response to the
crowds. Astonishingly, the day after the Coronation
brought no rest or relaxation, but found the Queen under-
taking a full programme, the presentation of 2,400 Coronation Medals to Commonwealth contingents in the garden
of the Palace in the morning, an investiture bestowing
knighthood on Sir David Fyfe, the Minister of Works, a
Coronation drive through north-west London that afternoon, a State Banquet that evening. Similar programmes
were observed on June 4th and 5th. June 6th brought the
excitement and gaiety of Derby Day and the defeat of the
Queen's horse Aureole by Gordon Richards on Pinza, a
defeat that nevertheless delighted the Queen because it

gave the popular Richards his first Derby win after twenty-eight attempts.

The following ten days were filled with every conceivable royal activity: a service of thanksgiving in St. Paul's, State drives, the Trooping the Colour, a Guildhall luncheon and the great Review of the Fleet at Spithead when the frigate H.M.S. *Surprise* served as the royal yacht, the *Britannia* having been launched by the Queen only three months earlier. Then came the thorough enjoyment of Royal Ascot and the traditional Windsor house party, endowed that year with a special quality of happiness and beauty by the inclusion of several of the Coronation maids-of-honour among the Queen's younger friends. It delighted the Queen herself that Princess Margaret was among the happiest of her guests. At the same time, the newspapers were now filling with speculation and rumour concerning the Princess's friendship with Group Captain Peter Townsend. This cast a small shadow on the Queen's hitherto unalloyed enjoyment of her Coronation season.

Any family discussions could however only be intermittent under the press of public events. Precisely twelve days after her Coronation, the Queen was in Edinburgh to attend a National Service at St. Giles's Cathedral and have the Honours of Scotland, the Scottish regalia, borne before her. Her Majesty had been crowned as Queen of England, Scotland being bound since the Act of Union to recognize as its sovereign the person crowned at Westminster, so a discussion as to whether the Queen was Elizabeth II of England but Elizabeth I of Scotland was irrelevant. The impressive ritual surrounding the Honours of Scotland was staged on the anniversary of the day when Robert

Bruce, greatest of Scottish kings, decisively defeated the English at Bannockburn.

There followed the Coronation visits to Northern Ireland and to Wales. On returning from Ulster the Queen smilingly said good-bye to Group Captain Townsend, who had been acting as her equerry and was being posted to Brussels, but both recognized the emotional questions that still hung in the balance. In contrast with this leave-taking was the occasion of particular pleasure for the Queen when she received the members of the 1953 Mount Everest Expedition at Buckingham Palace and knighted Colonel John Hunt, the leader, and Mr. Edmund Hillary, the news of whose conquest of the peak with Sherpa Tensing had come so propitiously on Coronation Day. The incongruity that a Presentation Party for overseas debutantes occurred that same afternoon could not be avoided, so allotted and crowded now was every minute of the Queen's time.

She was present at the International Horse Show on the same day that she also attended the Royal River Pageant on the Thames. She managed to snatch a Saturday afternoon at Sandown Park to watch Aureole running in the Eclipse Stakes, and some two weeks later she followed the fortunes at Goodwood of another royal horse, Choir Boy. But so great was the pressure of business that a Privy Council meeting had to be called at Goodwood House. If the old-fashioned raised their eyebrows, it was twenty-nine years to the day since King George V had held a Council at Goodwood, and the locale was in fact convenient to the Sussex peers and others attending.

Reviews, inspections, tours . . . so passed the Queen's crowded summer until she travelled north to Balmoral and, even there, questions continually arose on the wardrobe, organization, and personnel of the forthcoming Commonwealth tour. The problems of Mau Mau in Kenya, the new forms of government in Nigeria, the sad casualties of the Korean War, all demanded the Queen's attention. Each day, too, she allotted a little time to signing photographs. Hundreds of them awaited her signature before being sent to Embassies, Consulates, and British Service centres throughout the world. It was suggested that a rubber stamp duplicating her autograph could spare her effort. But the Queen deplored this disappointing substitution and signed so many photographs a day until the task was completed.

At seven-fifteen by Greenwich time on the morning of November 24th, 1953, the Queen awakened in her bunk aboard her B.O.A.C. plane, the Stratocruiser, *Canopus,* aware of the change of key in the engines and then the slight jolt of the landing. She had spent the night flying the Atlantic, the first Queen in history to do so. In London she had been cheered on her way by thousands, who again and again surged into the road on the route to the airport. The Queen and her husband had commenced the tour that was to take them through fourteen countries and cover some 50,000 miles in six months.

At Gander airfield, Newfoundland, it was now only 3.25 A.M., and as the engines were silenced the Queen heard the roar of a crowd singing "For she's a jolly good fellow!" She had first come to Canada as a Princess to be met with awed silence. Now she returned to the songs and greeting of people who had waited all night for her brief landing on Canadian soil. If the Queen had expected to rest in bed through a longer night she and the Duke now gave up all idea of sleep and hurriedly dressed. When they went to the door they found two Mounties whom they immediately recognized from their 1951 tour.

Such was the overture to a royal tour that an American has called "Possibly the most ambitious and certainly the most successful piece of public relations ever attempted." The tour had twice been arranged for King George VI, and when his elder daughter had made the third attempt in 1952 she had been recalled by her beloved father's death. "I will be back," she had said, on leaving Entebbe, but Prince Philip foresaw that to repeat that eastward-bound African journey might awaken too many painful memories. The revived tour was planned in reverse from west to east, and the briefest recital of the itinerary describes its speed and scope: "November 24th: Arrive Bermuda. 25th: Jamaica. 29th: Cristobal (Panama Canal). 30th: Depart Balboa. December 17th: Arrive Fiji. 20th: Tonga. 23rd: Arrive Auckland. January 30th: Depart New Zealand (Bluff). February 3rd: Arrive Sydney (Australia). April 1st: Depart Fremantle. 5th: Arrive Cocos Islands. 10th–21st: Visit Ceylon. . . ."

The stop at Gander was, in fact, only for refuelling. Seven hours later, summery, smiling, the Queen was visiting, as she said, "the first of my Parliaments Overseas." Bermuda boasts the oldest Commonwealth Parliament outside Westminster. After a day of shrilling and flag-waving children, beaming smiles in dusky faces, triumphal arches of flowers and seashells, the Queen was lulled to sleep by the croaking of bullfrogs. Next day she was up before 6 A.M. to head south in the *Canopus* to Jamaica, there to discover the wonderful gaiety and colour of the Caribbean and no doubt to think to herself, "Margaret must come here! Margaret must see this!"

The Legislative Council of the island had prescribed "perhaps a swim before lunch" and, after the miles of driving and the clusters of waving people, the royal couple were brought to Cottages 8 and 9, named "Memories" and "Kozy Korna," respectively blue-roofed and lemon-roofed, at the Silver Sands beach club. The swim in the warm ocean whetted their appetite for the lunch of kingfish mousse, Jamaica black crabs, roasted sucking pig, cold roast turkey, baked sweet ham, and coconut and banana ice cream, to name but some of the delicacies that were offered the Queen that day. Then came the 120-mile drive across the island to Kingston, through towns decked with paper arches and happy faces, with a tropical rainstorm thrown into the celebration, as if to freshen the air.

"Welcome, young Missus, our Queen" said printed slogans on the walls. "Welcome, welcome!" came the chant of the calypsos in every little town. Reporters travelling with the royal cavalcade noticed that on vacant parts of the road the Queen used a parasol but considerately laid it aside as soon as she saw people waiting to see her. Time and again the Queen's car paused to receive humble little offerings of flowers that were not on the schedule. When one old lady was passed inadvertently the car behind stopped to receive the little bunch of flowers she had ready. "Alice," said the Queen to her lady-in-waiting at the next stop, "did you thank the old lady? Did you ask her address? I'm so sorry we didn't see her in time. We will write and thank her."

A hundred such gestures touched and delighted Jamaicans in their royal three days. When at last their Queen was about to board the liner *Gothic* for departure, a man broke from the crowd and emulated Sir Walter Raleigh by flinging his coat at her feet. Although he was hustled away to the police station, the gleeful bulk of the island population felt that they would have shared his gesture.

The *Gothic* was a happy ship and the fourteen who sat down to dinner at the Royal table included the nucleus of the Queen's court: Sir Michael Adeane, who had succeeded Sir Alan Lascelles as Private Secretary; Colonel Charteris, the Assistant Private Secretary; Commander Colville, the Press Secretary; Lady Pamela Mountbatten and Lady Alice Egerton as ladies-in-waiting; Viscount Althorp, Deputy Controller of the Household, and Commander Michael Parker, the Duke of Edinburgh's Private Secretary. With these were Vice-Admiral Abel Smith, Flag Officer Royal Yachts; Captain David Aitchison of the *Gothic;* Surgeon-Commander D. D. Steele Perkins, and not least Wing-Commander Michael Cowan and Lieutenant Jeremy Hall, the Australian and New Zealander whose appointments as temporary equerries had been one of the tour's innovations. "A pleasant and compact little company," Captain Aitchison considered. A powerful long-range two-way radio—which incidentally electrified the stern of the ship when transmitting—kept in touch with affairs in London. In the morning, when it was tea-time in London, the Queen could talk to the royal nursery and hear of the day's doings, at least until the approaching International Date Line made *Gothic* time too far behind Greenwich. The afternoon saw boating parties to the escort cruiser H.M.S. *Sheffield* and later to the New Zealand cruiser *Black Prince.* But the Queen at last experienced a measure of lazy freedom, "running across the Pacific with the gentle trade wind behind us, blue sea, blue sky, and the temperature in the mid-seventies," as Captain Aitchison summed up. The lively games of deck hockey, which the Queen invariably watched, did not begin till four in the afternoon and the landfalls brought the gaiety, colour, and unexpected charm of holiday excursions ashore.

It had been planned, for instance, that the Queen and the Duke should motor across the Isthmus of Panama while the *Gothic* made the passage of the Canal. From the scheduled moment at 9.50 A.M. when the Queen inspected the smart American guard of honour on the dock, the royal party encountered an entirely unexpected and volcanic outburst of local enthusiasm. In Colon people left the pavement, in thousands, to surround the cars, half dispersing the procession by sheer weight of numbers, walking and running alongside, ringing handbells, waving flags, pressing from all sides. The Queen was continually alarmed lest anyone should be run down and the cars were constantly brought to a halt. Baton charges by the police, the terrific crack of maroons, the wild noise of rhythmic handclaps, the blare of motor-horns, heightened the garish scene. Cars cutting in from side-streets squeezed into the royal procession, and not all of them were left behind in the open country where the royal cars travelled at seventy miles an hour. In Balboa the Queen had fortunately been able to change to a closed car for the turmoil was soon repeated, with the extra emphasis of a torrential rainstorm that saw women waving and shrilling "Viva la Reina!" while the water streamed down their faces.

The crossing-the-Equator ceremony on the *Gothic* at the end of the week could not compete with these scenes, although the Duke acted as a vigorous and impartial lather boy and eventually the whole of Neptune's court—Neptune, judge, barber, lather boy and victims—threw one another into the pool. The Queen captured the hilarious fun with her amateur movie camera, so that it could be repeated on the screen at home to everyone's satisfaction.

Then another week of calm seas followed before the *Gothic* sailed into the entrance of Suva Harbour, where a pilot boat laden with flowers for the Queen was the first greeting of Fiji. Twenty outrigger canoes escorted the liner as she moved to her anchorage and guns thundered in royal salute as a deputation of Fijian chieftains came aboard to kneel ceremoniously before the Queen and present her with a whale's tooth in token of friendship and submission.

A request had gone forth that national dress should be worn, and not European. Accordingly, scarcely a pair of trousers was to be seen. Here, too, in the rites of welcome, the Queen was presented with a coconut bowl of kava, tasting like liquorice water mixed with soap, which she bravely drank at a gulp. Great was the acclaim. Then swaying files of flower-garlanded men and women trooped in the languorous rhythm of the "laka-laka," and after that a dance with clubs was so warlike that the Queen nearly jumped from her chair. That evening, as Her Majesty drove to a ball, two hundred grass-skirted torch-bearers ran alongside her car forming a lurid avenue of flame. Later, standing on a hotel balcony in the soft tropic night, she had the strange experience of hearing a crowd of 10,000 singing the Hallelujah Chorus. Stranger still was a visit made by a choir to the side of the *Gothic* at 5 A.M.

on the day of departure, there to sing songs of farewell, but softly, in order not to awaken their Sovereign.

Four hundred miles to the westward, Queen Salote of Tonga was waiting to greet the royal party. In London everyone affectionately remembers how this statuesque Queen captured the Coronation crowds by riding, smiling broadly, in an open carriage through the pouring rain. In Tonga the rain fell as the two Queens took their places in a carriage, and then stopped as soon as umbrellas were raised. The two royal ladies laughed together at this token. In a floral arch thirty-two small boys lay in hiding, ready to thrust out British and Tongan flags as the royal car passed beneath. Here, too, oddly the Duke of Edinburgh found himself riding in a London taxi, which Queen Salote had brought to Tonga as a Coronation souvenir; and here the centuries met, for Queen Elizabeth presently fed—or attempted to feed—a tortoise brought to the islands by Captain Cook when George III was on the throne.

The great feast—of which so much has been heard—was, in fact, two feasts. The first was served with pyramids of roast pig, shiploads of yams, coconuts and fruits on the lawns of Queen Salote's palace. The second was held the following day in a clearing outside her Polynesian-style palm-thatch-and-post country house. Even the background was lavishly prepared: banana trees heavily hung with fruit being uprooted elsewhere and transplanted to the clearing to give an effect. Here, too, were "sucking pigs by the dozen, cooked fish, raw fish, chickens in every state of dismemberment, tropical fruits . . ."

The visitors had been awakened that morning by a serenade of nose-flutes. It was a Sunday and the royal couple attended a service of two thousand people at the Methodist church, where the Duke read the lesson and the hymn-singing in Tongan was as melodious and fervent as anywhere in Wales.

Then came the farewells, with every member of Queen Elizabeth's suite garlanded with *leis;* the moment when a photographer cried out to Queen Salote, "Smile again please, Your Majesty. Your hand was hiding your face!" But for that timely interruption the Queen of Tonga, sad and excited, would have wept as she said good-bye to her protector Queen.

When the Queen arrived in the seaport of Auckland in drizzling rain on December 23rd an excited radio commentator "counted down" her steps on the gangway of the *Gothic,* "Five, four, three, two, ONE! She's here! She's in New Zealand!" Crammed in the streets, the people cheered at the mere announcement. Queen Elizabeth II was the first reigning British monarch to set foot in the Dominion. They cheered her vociferously up Queen Street to the Town Hall and cheered all the more when with rain still falling she rose to speak in her summer frock. "Give her an umbrella!" they shouted, and the Deputy Mayor hurriedly stripped off his raincoat. "Thank you, Sir Walter Raleigh!" said the Queen, loud enough for the microphones to catch and the delighted crowds acclaimed her again.

The tour was to take the royal couple north from Auckland to Waitangi on the Bay of Islands and south through every major centre of population to Bluff on the southern tip of South Island, but at the outset the Queen was grieved by a dreadful tragedy. A railway bridge collapsed into a flooded river, carrying with it a train crowded with

festive Christmas Eve passengers, and 166 people were
killed in the worst railway disaster in New Zealand history.
Swept away by the flood water, some bodies were found
fifty miles from the scene. The task of royalty, called
upon to take sorrowful note and yet to respond happily
to the crowds, is never more invidious than at times like
this. Talking to the Dean of Auckland, she said sympathetically that every family in New Zealand must know
someone affected by the crash, and so she called on a family
of survivors at a little house in an Auckland suburb. The
Duke of Edinburgh also flew to Wellington for the mass
funeral of the victims.

On Christmas Day, a children's choir sang carols for
the Queen on the lawn of Government House and then
Father Christmas himself appeared, New Zealand style, in
a coach drawn by four ponies, laden with gifts for the
Queen and the Duke, the royal children and the Queen's
staff. Thus the Queen received a diamond fernleaf brooch
from the women of Auckland; there was a doll in a wicker-
work pram for Princess Anne and an electric train set for
Prince Charles. Farther from her family than ever before,
the Queen heard their voices on sound-tape flown out
from England, and the children of Governor-General Sir
William Norrie shared her Christmas Day. For the first
time, too, Her Majesty spoke to her Commonwealth peoples from outside Britain. "The Commonwealth bears no
resemblance to the empires of the past. It is an entirely
new conception built on the highest qualities of the spirit
of man: friendship, loyalty, and the desire for freedom
and peace. . . ."

In all, the Queen made twenty-eight speeches in New
Zealand, including the "Speech from the Throne" in the

Parliament House in Wellington when she wore her fabulous Coronation gown.

Before opening Parliament in Wellington the Queen typically broke into time assigned for "rest" to join a rehearsal. The Cook Strait was then comfortably flown and the South Island of New Zealand gave a welcome not a whit less memorable, moving and impressive than the North. Here, too, by mournful coincidence, the Queen was privately saddened on arrival, for she heard that her chief steward on the *Gothic* had suffered a cerebral haemorrhage.

The curtain on the Queen's visit to New Zealand was, however, rung down by a little harbour tug, noted in the port of Bluff for her prolific capacity for producing smoke. Scheduled to aid in turning the *Gothic,* the skipper assured the authorities that he had laid in twenty bags of special smokeless fuel to be ready for the Queen.

The dreary wharf was turned into a flower garden. The bands played. The people cheered. The Queen and the Duke went to the saluting place above the *Gothic*'s bridge. But black smoke from the tug billowed across the liner. The smokeless fuel loosened the soot in the funnels with dire effect and soon neither saluting base nor Royalty could be seen.

Greeted by thousands of small craft in the harbour and even by enthusiasts on water skis, the Queen first set foot in Australia on February 3rd, 1954. In the next two months she was to travel 2,500 miles by road, 900 miles by train and 10,000 miles by plane, making thirty-five different flights. In fifty-eight days she was to have six days and seven half-days free. One intensive two-day programme, it was calculated, entailed her being on her feet for twenty hours. The full list of the arrangements occupied a bulky volume, which irreverently came to be known as the Black Bible, not only for the hue of its binding but also for its almost brutal demands. Australia wanted to outdo New Zealand. Melbourne hoped to outshine Sydney. The sum total was put by an imaginative statistician as 102 speeches made and 200 heard, 162 anthems and 190 gifts, 4,800 handshakes and 2,500 curtseys, and this seems an underestimate.

Future historians may look back on these marathons and be astounded at the youthful energies and royal professionalism that enabled the Queen and her husband to withstand fatigue. Her Majesty had so conserved her time and perfected her methods of physical relaxation that she came through—indeed, in high spirits—days that left tough naval men worn out. She could show exasperation with official stupidity and yet her vigilant thoughtfulness for others sometimes startled even the members of her suite. After the rigours of her first day in Sydney, after enduring for some ten hours the noise of a million people who were "letting it rip," when her car finally returned to Government House she did not omit to turn to her chauffeur and say, "Thank you, driver. This has been a trying day for you."

In Canberra, when presenting new military colours, when officers were intent on the observance of the correct drill and spectators were intent on the royal lady, only the Queen noticed a drummer-boy swaying in the scorching sun of the parade ground. The cadet, though near collapse, was determined not to break ranks and the Queen alone saw that something was wrong and gently pointed him out to the Commandant, who signalled an ambulance.

Although the swift recuperation of youth was on her side, the Queen was losing weight before she began touring South Australia, and Miss Macdonald was rumoured to be taking in her dresses. From the western horizon, too, developed a small cloud that threatened the entire future of the tour. The incidence of polio was assuming epidemic proportions, and a woman who had been visiting Perth had shaken the Queen's hand in Canberra while innocently carrying the disease. The Queen wished to continue the tour, but she could not disregard her doctors. Alas, assemblies of children could no longer be permitted. Under restrictions, the Queen continued her journey to Perth and Fremantle, but it was arranged that she should not shake hands with anyone, indoor receptions were cancelled and mingling with large crowds was to be avoided. The officers and men of the *Gothic*, moreover, submitted to quarantine; the Queen arranged to sleep only on board and to eat only food supplied from the ship. To allay public alarm these restrictions were only partly repealed at the time. An insulated ice-cream wagon was used to take hot meals to the royal couple when they were unavoidably ashore, and if dishes were tepid they never complained.

The royal ship finally sailed from Fremantle on April 1st. The last farewells were made on the dock without handshakes. From her sitting-room on board, as the *Gothic* steamed into the Indian Ocean, the Queen broadcast her parting message, "The Crown is a human link between all peoples who owe allegiance to me," she said. "An al-

legiance of mutual love and respect and never of com-
pulsion. . . ."

But perhaps the last word can be given to an Australian
woman who wrote to her daughter, never thinking that her
words would see print, "Inspired as she herself is, she has
been an inspiration and hope to everyone. No one has
anything but good to say of her and are puzzled (even the
hardbitten) at the effect she has on them. Yes, I have seen
her. It has been easy for everyone to see her, and she has
been safe, loved and considered. . . ."

CHAPTER IX

THE FIRST HAZARDS

WHEN THE QUEEN and the Duke of Edinburgh returned
to London on Saturday, May 15th, 1954, they had
circumnavigated the globe in 173 days. Her Majesty was
the first Queen to travel round the world. The homecoming was beautifully staged, with two hundred jets flying
overhead, the Queen's chief Ministers waiting at the pier,
and a Sovereign's Escort for the procession to the Palace.

Characteristically, after a weekend of exchanging news
with the Queen Mother and Princess Margaret, the Queen
immediately plunged into business. A sherry party for the
Cabinet and Opposition leaders, itself an innovation, was
held at the Palace on the Monday. The following day the
Queen presided over a lengthy meeting of the Prince's
Council of the Duchy of Cornwall, and the next day saw
a welcome-home luncheon by the City of London. "Out
of the lively interest in Britain is spreading something
new, something which holds great promise for the future,"
said the Queen, as she summed up her journey. "It was to
learn more of the peoples and countries over which I have

been called to reign that I set out, and also to try to bring
to them the personal reality of the Monarchy. . . . The
structure and framework of monarchy could easily stand
as an archaic and meaningless survival. We have received
visible and audible proof that it is living in the hearts of
the people."

The Queen's grandfather, King George V, had returned
from the Delhi Durbar with a new self-confidence and a
new conception of the majesty of his office and the magni-
tude of his responsibilities. In the same way, to the young
couple sailing in remote oceans, time and distance presented
the immense ever-present problem of the Monarchy in fresh
perspective. The Queen was neither flattered nor deceived
by frenzied reporting and crowd hysteria. She recognized
the dross, but could frequently be touched to tears by the
genuine. With her special humility, the Queen could feel
that every impassioned welcome was not so much for herself as for her queenhood, her embodiment of an abiding
link with history, the Crown itself at once an emblem and
a hope.

Now the years of accession, coronation, and of presentation to the Commonwealth lay behind: but what lay
ahead? In that early summer of 1954 one may suppose
that the Queen and Prince Philip looked forward to private family hopes which were not to be immediately fulfilled, but they also anticipated eighteen months of quiet
and tentative experiment in the consolidation and strength-
ening of their office.

One may use the plural "their" in the sense of a most
intimate fraternity of interests and working companionship. Whatever the conventional picture of the solitude
of her high position, there were few problems which Her

Majesty could not discuss with her husband, gaining the benefit of his lively mind and fuller experience. While investigating and expanding to the full every useful activity he could undertake as consort, Philip's direct influence on the Throne was officially nothing and unofficially limitless. It was a fiction to pretend that the Queen could consult and take the advice of her Private Secretary without equally seeking advice from her husband.

One of the documents signed by the Queen while overseas had, indeed, been the new Regency Act appointing the Duke of Edinburgh to become Regent in the event of her death while the child succeeding to the Throne was under eighteen. This enactment had only been made after consultation and agreement with Princess Margaret, who stepped down one remove in line of regency. To the degree that the Act enhanced the status and responsibility of the Duke of Edinburgh, it diminished the responsibilities of the Princess, who still faced and deferred her final decision on whether she should marry Group Captain Peter Townsend.

If not a sorrow, it was certainly a matter of acute concern and perplexity to the Queen at this time that her younger sister should continue to contemplate marriage with a man who had been concerned in divorce, a marriage that the Church of England would not recognize and which the Queen could not therefore constitutionally approve. The opportunities for thought and quiet discussion during the cruise of the *Gothic* had shed no fresh light on this cruel dilemma. So often in childhood the elder sister had said with playful resignation, "I don't know what we are going to do with Margaret," and now the fates had presented her with this problem in its saddest and most

hurtful terms. Deeply anxious for her sister's happiness, it
was but human for the Queen to hope that the emotional
crisis might perhaps disperse. The departure of Group
Captain Townsend to Brussels had afforded the Princess
an opportunity of calm and untrammelled consideration.
But Princess Margaret had apparently suffered no change
of heart in the summer of 1954 and objective observers
could not discount this shadow on the Queen's serenity.

In 1944 King George VI had instituted a new system
of appointments for Equerries of Honour, temporarily
placing in service close to his person young men of dis-
tinguished royal records, and Wing Commander Peter
Townsend was one of the first so chosen. In active command of No. 85 Fighter Squadron his heroism in the
Battle of Britain and its aftermath caused him to be re-
peatedly decorated at Buckingham Palace, until one day
the King, presenting him with a bar to his D.S.O., exclaimed, "What, you again?"

From 1945 onwards it sometimes happened that the discreet and personable airman was called upon to escort the
two Princesses. In April, 1946, Princess Elizabeth included
him in her theatre party when they went to see *The First
Gentleman*. Some three months later, Townsend oblig-
ingly squired them to a local cinema in Edinburgh. Early
in 1947 Wing Commander Peter Townsend and Lieuten-
ant-Commander Peter Ashmore, of the Royal Navy, were
appointed equerries on the royal tour to South Africa. The
two Princesses were cast frequently into the company of
the "two Peters," as they were amiably known, as riding
and dancing partners. Princess Elizabeth may have found
more interest in Peter Ashmore, who was the same age as

Prince Philip and had served on destroyers. As it happened, Ashmore was a bachelor and seven years younger than Townsend, yet ironically it was not the unmarried Peter Ashmore but the older married man who chiefly engaged Princess Margaret's attentions.

In 1950 the King appointed Group Captain Townsend Deputy Master of the Household and offered the thirty-six-year-old airman and his family the grace and favour occupancy of Adelaide Cottage in Windsor Great Park. Group Captain Townsend strove to find a balance between his devotion to the King and Queen and the responsibilities of his wife and family. His war-time marriage was, however, destined not to last, and in December, 1952, he divorced his wife. The suit was undefended.

It was unfortunate that rumours concerning Princess Margaret and Townsend should have broken in the British Press at the time of the Coronation. As with King Edward VIII and Mrs. Simpson, the first wavelets of gossip rippled from America and the Continent and crashed across the shores of Britain in a fury of speculation. The Duke of Edinburgh disliked this midsummer storm intensely, just as he disliked anything that could diminish or threaten the dignity of the Crown. The Queen herself could only urge her sister to have patience, perhaps hoping that a diplomatic way could be found through the impasse. Then her discovery of the West Indies on her Commonwealth tour led to the tactful and wise suggestion that Princess Margaret should also visit the Indies in 1955 as a special envoy.

Three sunny months in the Caribbean, in reality, wrought a sea change in her sister's sensibilities that was not at first apparent. The Queen noted with joy the wonderful welcome home accorded to the Princess in the City of London, where crowds gathered around the Mansion House to cheer her loudly. The Lord Mayor, Sir Seymour Howard, had drafted his speech with exceptional care and was prepared to point a moral. The British Royal Family, he could say remindfully, "is the family of perfect example for every other family in every part of Her Majesty's realm, of right standards, sound principles, true relationship, and a way of life approved by all. It is the most hardworking of all families in the discharge of its national duties and its task of unifying the British partnership of peoples." His words expressed the crux of the schism between private affections and royal responsibilities.

The Queen, of course, realized that when the Princess reached the age of twenty-five she would be free under the Royal Marriages Act to marry without her consent. Throughout the summer of 1955 a series of newspaper interviews with Group Captain Townsend required precisely that insensitive thickness of skin that from time to time seems to be expected of the Royal Family. It was not until October 31st, 1955, that Princess Margaret issued her statement of renunciation, "I would like it to be known that I have decided not to marry Group Captain Townsend. I have been aware that, subject to my renouncing my rights of succession, it might have been possible for me to contract a civil marriage. But, mindful of the Church's teachings that Christian marriage is indissoluble, and conscious of my duty to the Commonwealth, I have resolved to put these considerations before others. . . ."

The high modern incidence of divorce made it necessary in any case for the protocol *vis-à-vis* divorce to be more closely defined and explained. King George V had eased the rules of precedent when he ceased to prohibit the admission of innocent parties to the Royal Enclosure at Ascot. There were, in fact, royal relatives, such as Princess Marie-Louise, whose marriages had been annulled, and other blameless but divorced persons who now held positions of authority within the Royal Household itself. The impending retirement of Sir Winston Churchill and the probability of Sir Anthony Eden as his successor implied that the Queen would have as her Prime Minister a party to a divorce action. Considerations of divorce had not prevented the Queen and her husband from privately dining with a divorced actor, although the Honours Committee long withheld knighthood from another deserving but divorced figure of the stage. Consultations were held with Church leaders, and ample time was given for each decision to be reconsidered, before the Lord Chamberlain freshly defined the restrictions. Guilty parties to divorces could not be invited to functions held by the Queen within her royal palaces, and the yacht *Britannia* ranked as a palace in this respect. Innocent parties could be received and persons in public office could be received on account of that office. Similarly it was announced that the divorce rules would henceforth be applied not to the Royal Enclosure, but to the Queen's Lawn, where admission would be only by invitation. By this modification, the Queen also effectively disposed of the criticism that tickets to the Royal Enclosure, which had to be paid for, provided ready access to the Royal Family by money alone.

The Queen's close regard to criticism is now well known, and indeed criticism is seldom ignored until Her Majesty has made up her mind that it is false or overstated.

Thus when spokesmen of the League Against Cruel Sports called the Queen "our worst enemy," she did not abandon deer-stalking, although she has come to prefer the movie-camera to the gun. With the passage of ten years it has become evident that all cogent arguments have been read with close attention. Writing in 1952, one critic had expressed the hope that the Crown could be brought into closer touch with the leaders of thought and especially men of letters. As if in direct answer, the Queen's private round table luncheons were inaugurated at Buckingham Palace in May, 1956, bringing to her side authors and artists, leaders of thought and education, industrial and trade union leaders, musicians, scientists, journalists, and judges, worthy representatives indeed of every section of British life. If the inclusion of clowns and professional footballers seemed questionable, one could recall that forty years earlier actresses, musicians, and singers could not be presented at Court, unless retired and utterly respectable. If the impatient could point to delay between the criticism and the reform, we may judge that the Queen was mistrustful of her own youth, and we must remember that in such a traditional institution as the Monarchy the smallest change can not be made without great care and consideration.

Sir Charles Petrie, one of the Queen's wisest and fairest critics, expressed the hope that Queen Elizabeth II would find much to remedy in the presentation of debutantes at Court and, as we know, the decision to end these functions came in November, 1957. In this, the Queen was following a lead given by her father, who had already reduced many evening presentations to afternoon parties on the plea of economy.

The King had also been a firm believer in the *esprit de corps* of kings. Although the war, cutting into his reign, prevented him from receiving and returning the State Visits which he would otherwise have known, the hostilities equally enabled him to offer true hospitality to at least five exiled monarchs. In his final well-balanced criticism Sir Charles Petrie also stressed the continuing value of international monarchist solidarity on which both Queen Victoria and King Edward VII had laid such emphasis. Sure enough, in the third year of her reign, the Queen received a State Visit from the King and Queen of Sweden, her uncle and aunt by marriage, and from the Emperor Haile Selassie of Ethiopia. Less formally, Her Majesty entertained President Auriol of France, Prince Bernhard of the Netherlands and his three daughters, King Feisal of Iraq, and the King of Jordan. Then in 1955 a State Visit was paid to Her Majesty by President Creveira Lopes and Senhora Lopes of Portugal and the Queen received the Shah of Persia, among others. In June the Queen made the first State Visit of her own reign to her kinsman King Haakon of Norway.

The Queen and her husband sailed from Rosyth aboard the *Britannia,* but not before Her Majesty had launched and named the Canadian liner *Empress of Britain* on Clydeside. Sailing past the south Norwegian coast, the fiords reminded the Queen vividly of New Zealand, and since it was Midsummer Eve the traditional bonfires of that celebration seemed to blaze in welcome.

King Haakon of Norway had visited England for the Coronation in his own royal yacht *Norge*, and at that time the representatives of the Queen of England had no better craft in which to greet him than a police launch. For half a century the old royal yacht *Victoria and Albert* had been kept upright with six hundred tons of concrete ballast and in any case she was no longer seaworthy. That was why King George VI had sailed to South Africa in the cramped quarters of a battleship and Queen Elizabeth returned from Australia with a cargo of frozen meat.

The new royal yacht *Britannia* was finally ordered from John Brown's Clydeside yard in 1951, and she had been designed by the Admiralty so that she could be rapidly converted into a hospital ship if necessary. "The late King felt most strongly, as I do, that a yacht was a necessity and not a luxury," said the Queen at the launching. Certainly no more impressive form of showing the flag for the ruler of a great seafaring nation and the head of a world-wide Commonwealth could be devised. Nevertheless the vessel was to be constantly criticized in Parliament, in attacks ranging from the cost of every refit to its romantic use for Princess Margaret's honeymoon. Every minor modification, every brushload of gold leaf to the line on the hull, brought insinuations of extravagance. After the voyage to Norway in June, the Queen and her family embarked again in August to sail around the western and northern coasts of Scotland to Balmoral, and the yacht was used as a base while the Queen and her husband made an official tour of western Wales and official visits to the Isle of Man. Yet carping reproaches were heard because the yacht served for royal recreation as well as duty.

Princess Anne, learning to swim and fast catching up with her brother, celebrated her fifth birthday at Balmoral. In 1955 the children were, in fact, growing up sufficiently for their schooling to be a recurrent topic of family discussion. The young Duke of Cornwall was making good progress under his governess, Miss Katharine Peebles, but both parents wished his education to be shared as soon as possible with other children. But if Prince Charles attended classes at a day school, would his teachers suffer the embarrassment of constant publicity? The Queen decided to solicit the support of the Press, and Commander Colville, her Press Secretary, addressed a letter to the Newspaper Proprietors' Association, ". . . a certain amount of the Duke of Cornwall's instruction will take place outside his home. . . . The Queen trusts that His Royal Highness will be able to enjoy this in the same way as other children can. . . ."

In general, this direct approach brought a sympathetic response, probably giving the Queen an illusion that reliance on the good faith of the public might always be reciprocated. Fortified by this pleasant belief, the Queen ventured a new experiment when she attended a fair at Abergeldie Castle to raise funds for a new vestry at the Crathie parish church. The Queen hoped to tend a stall without the occasion rising above the parochial. The eve of Princess Margaret's twenty-fifth birthday, however, saw the Press of the world encamped around Balmoral, and unaccustomed August holidaymakers by the thousand far outnumbered the staid and sensible local folk. The result was pandemonium. Women cried out in panic as they found themselves jammed against the temporary crush barriers. Children fell and dresses and jackets were ripped, while the whole crowd crushed and wavered. Those at the front cried out "Don't push!" while those behind "clawed their way forward" and disappointed people outside the tent slipped round to the back and began pulling down the canvas to see inside. The experiment was not repeated.

Much earlier, in April, in dining with Sir Winston and Lady Churchill at No. 10 Downing Street on the occasion of her Prime Minister's retirement, the Queen was not setting a precedent, for King George VI and his Queen had dined in Downing Street with both the Baldwins and Chamberlains.

Sir Winston Churchill's retirement from office was muted by a newspaper strike. Sir Winston had on occasions named Sir Anthony Eden as his "eventual successor," but this was said only at meetings of the Conservative Party in referring to leadership of the party and the legacy had no reference to the post of Prime Minister. Although Sir Anthony had acted for over three years as "deputy" Prime Minister, this office held no actual validity in the Constitution. Sir Winston Churchill drove to Buckingham Palace and tendered his resignation at 4.30 P.M. on April 5th, but the Queen did not send for Sir Anthony Eden within an hour or two, as had been expected. She was under no obligation to consult Sir Winston about his successor, nor was she constitutionally required to seek advice. Firmly to lend observance to her royal prerogative, the Queen allowed the night to pass and did not send for Sir Anthony Eden until eleven o'clock the following morning.

Change was in the air. For the first time in her reign the Queen granted a dissolution of Parliament for a general election, and opened her own First Parliament, the fifteenth of the century, after the Conservatives had been returned with an increased majority of sixty. She had evidently hoped to open Parliament with the usual panoply of State, but in the midst of a rail and dock strike, decided to drive to Westminster in a closed car. The Trooping the Colour was also cancelled.

On a July day the Queen took the salute of Sir Anthony Eden's old regiment, the King's Royal Rifles, at Winchester, and afterwards she received the Prime Minister in audience in the Deanery. In those quiet surroundings he told her of the thermonuclear undercurrents of the Geneva Conference and of the invitation to London for the following year of Marshal Bulganin and Mr. Khrushchev.

CHAPTER X

FROM LAGOS TO STOCKHOLM

M Y HUSBAND AND I are regular air travellers and we are
looking forward to our first departure from these
buildings next month." So said the Queen when she inaugurated the new central terminal area of London airport
late in 1955. A few weeks later, on January 27th, 1956, as
she and her husband stepped from their car in the chilly
winter dusk at London airport, Nigeria immediately
stretched out her arms to welcome them with the lilt of
leopardskin drums and the rhythm of African strings, with
men and women in colourful robes and headdresses swaying and singing. The London Nigerian contingent was out
in full force for the leave-taking. Amid their infectious
gaiety, the Queen was perhaps untroubled by the thought
that her *Atalanta* aircraft was the very plane in which she
had tragically flown home to her Accession. Now Captain
R. C. Parker, the chief pilot, could report a clear sky and
a tail wind for the first of her separate visits as the Commonwealth Queen.

The plane took off at 4 P.M. and at 11.30 it touched

down in Tripoli, completing in seven-and-a-half hours the journey that had taken fifteen days after the Commonwealth tour when the Queen returned from Africa by sea.

Romantically that night the Queen was flown over the Sahara while she slept. She breakfasted as the plane flew over the lush greens of what was already Nigeria, and punctually at 9 A.M. the royal couple stepped out at Lagos airport into the humidity of the near-Equator.

The 35,000,000 people of the Federation of Nigeria had only recently passed through the throes of self-determination. But they were still two years away from self-government. Though then ranking as the largest British colony and protectorate, Nigeria had never before been visited by the reigning sovereign. Forty-four years earlier her grandparents, King George V and Queen Mary, had attended the Delhi Durbar, a formal reception of native princes, which was to be long remembered in Imperial history as an unqualified success. In Nigeria the Durbar at Kaduna was to spread before the Queen a pageantry of homage no less memorable. Eight thousand chiefs, emirs, and warriors came to do her honour with medieval richness and splendor. Almost at the same moment Sir Anthony Eden was addressing the United States Senate and House of Representatives in Washington, D.C. "Everywhere through our Commonwealth and Empire nations are growing up. This places a heavy responsibility upon the parent. He has to be sure that patience is shown, that guidance is given, that experience is passed—as a warning but not as a command. At this very moment Her Majesty the Queen is in Nigeria, where dwell more than thirty millions of her people with elected legislators and African Ministers, and the spontaneous enthusiasm of her welcome will have shown how the people really feel. . . ."

To the Queen this visit was a medley of the colourful past and of modern progress. Two Nigerians had been appointed as equerries, and three months of preparation had seen a stream of visitors to Buckingham Palace who could further Her Majesty's interest in one phase or another of Nigerian affairs. As it turned out, no one told her about the dust of Lagos. The rusting bridge into the city had been painted blue and silver; the civic rubbish piles sterilized and top-dressed with cinders; the Queen's bedroom at Government House air-conditioned and cooled to such an extent that until the thermostat was adjusted, flowers began to wither with cold. But the jumping, dancing welcome of the Nigerian crowds threw up clouds of ochre dust that reddened the Queen's parasol and much of her frock and stained the Duke of Edinburgh's white drill. The Queen took it all in good part. Some crowds have a screaming mania; some are awed and silent; some are touchers, seeking to touch the royal car or the royal person.

The colourful people of Lagos were both dancers and hat-doffers. Having read that hats should be removed in the presence of royalty, many had bought hats purely for the courtesy of taking them off. Headgear was indeed important. The President of the Lagos Town Council wore a crown of gold fabric. The Nigerian Minister of Labour affected a boater with a foot-high spray of feathers. His colleague, the Minister of Communications, wore a cap studded with jewels. King Mingi of Membe preferred a crown in ermine and velvet: there were crowns in bamboo, bone and beads, recalling the days at 145 Piccadilly when two little girls played at Kings and Queens.

Her Majesty spent four days in Lagos. There was an evening when ten thousand masked and painted dancers passed before her, some whirling on stilts twelve feet high, others juggling huge axes with unexampled skill and peril, a foretaste of the pageantry when the Queen flew north to Kaduna, the capital of the northern peoples. Here, with fanfares of ancient trumpets thousands of horsemen greeted her in an avenue five miles long, wearing turbans and robes of every variety and hue; their horses caparisoned as if from the Arabian Nights. The next day brought the Durbar and, as her grandmother Queen Mary had done in India, the Queen returned the salute of her peoples by appearing in brocaded silk, ermine, and diamonds at nine o'clock in the morning.

The thudding drums had awakened the town five hours earlier. Fifty thousand spectators were gathered around the Durbar ground, some in rows of white gowns in the stands, others massed in human walls of white and ebony. "The Field of the Cloth of Gold must have looked something like this. As the movement of forming-up began, the morning sun caught the glitter of thousands of spears and sword blades, and picked out the brocaded garments," an English eyewitness recorded. There passed before the Queen's eyes "an unreal procession of horses and men which might have emerged from the mists of African history . . . Emirs and great chieftains, spearsmen and archers, clowns and tumblers and half-naked pagans gathered in all their barbarous magnificence. . . ."

Every mounted chief was surrounded by retainers, and the great pageant ended with wave on wave of Jari and Zaria horsemen, in plumed helmets, robes and armour, charging at full gallop across the ground, yelling and shrieking, to pull up in clouds of eddying sand within yards of the Queen.

After this unforgettable week, Queen Elizabeth and Prince Philip flew to the coolness of Jos, in the hills, where a bungalow had been prepared for them. Here they worshipped on Sunday in a tin-roofed church where, suitably enough, the floor was spread with a length of the Coronation carpet used in Westminster Abbey. The royal couple then flew over jungle and swamp to Enugu, the capital of Eastern Nigeria, in a region of coal and tin mines. Here, too, the Queen had agreed to drive some miles out of her way to visit a leper settlement. It is not generally known that the Queen and the Queen Mother have adopted several leper children, paying for all their medical and other needs. At Oji River the Queen saw and was seen by a thousand patients, visiting all the compounds and classes, compassionate and unflinching for those unfortunate people who had perhaps arrived too late for treatment. This visit lessened the Africans' exaggerated fear of contagion.

Next the Queen and her husband travelled westward by train to visit Ibadan, largest all-African city of the continent. "The Queen continually broke away from white residents to talk to Nigerians and constantly broke through the difficulties of race and custom." For this after all was what she had come there to do.

After three weeks at home, the Queen again flew south, this time to join the *Britannia* in a short Mediterranean cruise. The journey was a rare impromptu; Prince Philip had been attending Fleet exercises, and he suggested that the Queen should fly out so that he might show her Corsica and Sardinia. There is nothing more disappointing than a cruise for the sunshine when the sun refuses to appear. The Queen had the fun of going ashore with Princess Alexandra of Kent to eat spaghetti in tiny restaurants and stroll amid the fishing-nets on picturesque wharfs. But the rain fell and the wind blew, and perhaps it was just as well that Princess Margaret had not joined this forlorn adventure.

The sisters were together at the Grand National—the steeplechase that year saw the disastrous failure of the Queen Mother's Devon Loch—and they were both at Badminton for the Horse Trials. The Queen spent her thirtieth birthday quietly at Windsor with her husband for the Queen Mother and Princess Margaret had a prior engagement at Holkham Hall, in Norfolk, to attend a wedding. The young photographer who arranged the wedding groups caught and held Princess Margaret's amused attention. His name was Mr. Antony Armstrong-Jones.

Meeting later, the two sisters had many topics to share. The Queen had invited Marshal Bulganin and Mr. Khrushchev to tea at Windsor. Princess Margaret could beg her sister to come and see her favourite show, the witty *Cranks*, a revue for which Mr. Armstrong-Jones had done some of the photographic scenery. The Queen could now recognize her sister's revived gaiety and good spirits and was content. Nevertheless, when the Queen and the Duke of Edinburgh sailed on the *Britannia* in June for their State Visit to Sweden, it was arranged that the Princess should fly and join them for the private part of the visit that followed. The King and Queen of Sweden are, of course, uncle and aunt of Prince Philip and, knowing the tastes of their niece-in-law, arranged that her visit coincided with the equestrian events of the Olympic Games.

When the *Britannia* approached Stockholm, mist veiled all the holms and islets, but fortunately the sun was shining as the yacht reached her anchorage and the guns boomed in salute. For the Queen the magic of that arrival was enhanced by the ornate blue and gold royal barge, manned by eighteen oarsmen, in which she travelled the last half-mile to the bridges and docks of the city. Here were the waiting crowds who were to applaud her throughout her stay. The "Venice of the North" cannot but charm the visitor, not least when decked with the flowers and festivities of a State Visit in summer.

For the ensuing private stay the Queen made her headquarters on the *Britannia*, visiting the Olympic stadium each day. And she enjoyed splashing through mud and rain to see as much as possible of the endurance phase of the Three Day event. Her horse, Countryman, completed the twenty-two-mile course in spite of a fall at one of the thirty-three fences and the British team most appropriately won the Gold Medal. The following week the Queen took pride in showing her Olympic colour movie to her Ascot guests.

This 1956 Royal Ascot also saw the Queen's horse, Alexander, win the Royal Hunt Cup in a photo-finish. This was not the Queen's greatest racing year, but she ended the season fourth among the winning owners and the following year was to find Her Majesty at the top of the list. Altogether, the three years 1956-59 saw her exceed £125,-000 in stake winnings. In the complete relaxation of racing —and in the hobby of breeding racehorses—the Queen could firmly follow her own judgement and indeed often vindicate it against the cautious advice of professional experts.

After President Nasser had seized the Suez Canal the Queen was criticized for signing a military call-up at Goodwood races. In point of fact as the crisis developed, the Queen had inquired whether she should stay in London and had been reassured. Among the practical steps to be urgently taken was a Proclamation calling out the Army Reserve, and the Queen properly agreed to approve the draft text at the earliest possible moment. As soon as the document was ready, it was therefore rushed to her private rooms in the Duke of Richmond's box. The next day the Proclamation was formally signed at a Privy Council at Arundel Castle. Wherever she had been, the Queen could have done no more.

The Queen, like many of her peoples, found 1956 a seesaw of good news and bad. In January a diminution of the royal prestige came when the Sudan proclaimed itself an independent republic without Commonwealth affiliations. In March, however, the new nation of Pakistan was proclaimed a republic within the Commonwealth. In February the referendum in Malta resulted in a vote in favour of integration with Britain, while, the following month, the bloodshed in Cyprus began gravely increasing. So events went, and then in July the seizure of the Suez Canal presented the Queen with a crisis.

At the time of Suez, King Feisal of Iraq was concluding a State Visit to London; his successful *rapport* with the Palace was based on youth and sincerity as well as friendship, and the Queen left him in no doubt of the firmness with which this challenge would be met. Elizabeth II met nearly every statesman whom the crisis brought to London and, as Sir Ivor Jennings has said, "To express a doubt is often more helpful than to formulate a criticism; to throw in a casual remark is often more helpful than to write a memorandum."

The Monarchy has progressed from the days when Queen Victoria would indignantly assert that "never would she consent" to this or that proposal, only to give her formal signature at the requisite moment. Queen Elizabeth II was at the centre of events; the documents marshalled in her boxes were more numerous than usual until arrangements for the conference of twenty-two nations in London passed the problem to international authority. In September, Mr. Menzies, the Australian Prime Minister, stopped over at Balmoral to tell her of his talks with President Nasser in Egypt, but his report was not one of success, and all the looming anxieties still remained.

At this juncture the Duke of Edinburgh departed on his 1956-57 world tour. The 38,000-mile trip was to take him away from home for four months. In nine years of marriage, even during his Malta naval service, the Queen had never before been deprived of his companionship for so long. His earlier solo visit to Canada had occupied only three weeks. Yet it was consoling that the tour, from Kenya and Ceylon, Malaya and Australia, New Zealand and the Gambia served to remind the world afresh of the cohesion and strength in partnership of the Commonwealth.

In the Duke's absence, Princess Margaret rode with the Queen for the State Opening of Parliament and in effect assisted as her chief aide at the Palace luncheon parties. With the Christmas broadcast from Sandringham, however, the Queen could strive again to underline the inner motive of her husband's travels, "We are the solid facts beneath the words and phrases, we are the solid flesh-and-blood links which draw the Commonwealth under the Crown. . . ." However, she missed the reassurance of her husband's company as she faced the microphone. She was widely criticized for allowing the annual speech to become repetitive. It was to be drastically reorganized the following year, as we shall see.

Moreover, the Christmas festivities were no sooner over when Her Majesty was forced to make one of the foremost constitutional decisions of her reign without her husband's company and moral support.

The Queen knew and amply sympathized with the intense strain that Suez had placed on her Ministers. She knew, too, that her Prime Minister, Sir Anthony Eden, was being impeded by recurrent attacks of ill health. Early in January, 1957, he inquired whether the Queen would receive his wife and himself, at Sandringham. Before dinner he repeated the doctors' opinion that his illness would increase in intensity, and that this could not be ignored without detriment to her service.

Queen Elizabeth said that in the circumstances she would go to London the next day and it was agreed that Sir Anthony Eden should tender his resignation at the Palace in the evening. His action provoked a maelstrom of speculation. Two foremost figures seemed to have almost equal claims as Britain's next Prime Minister, Mr. Harold Macmillan, Chancellor of the Exchequer, and Mr. R. A. Butler, Lord Privy Seal and Leader of the House of Commons. Both were close on balance of merits, each had a considerable body of opponents and neither commanded the unanimous support of the Conservative Party. It was for the Queen alone to decide. Her Private Secretary, Sir

Michael Adeane, had no experience of any similar dilemma. The Queen sought the advice of Sir Winston Churchill and the Marquess of Salisbury, Lord President of the Council, among others, and these senior statesmen dutifully attended at the Palace on January 10th. In his memoirs Sir Anthony Eden gives no indication that the Queen sought his advice that day, although she no doubt had asked for his opinions at Sandringham. The deliberations continued through the morning of the 10th. As on the occasion when Sir Winston Churchill retired from office the Queen allowed precisely 18½ hours to pass before she showed her mind and sent for the new Prime Minister. Mr. Harold Macmillan was occupied only twenty minutes in being received and offered the post of Prime Minister and First Lord of the Treasury and, within the hour, the Queen drove out of the Palace and returned by car to her country home.

CHAPTER XI

GATE OF THE 'THIRTIES

T HE WINTER OF SEPARATION from her husband dragged for the Queen. In spite of her usual preoccupations Her Majesty visited Cumberland to open the world's first nuclear power station at Calder Hall; she was at the Bolshoi Ballet's presentation of *Giselle;* the television cameras were privileged to study her when she presided over an Army dinner in the Great Hall of the Royal Hospital, Chelsea. Among the visitors at the Palace was a deputation from Virginia to ask if a stop at Jamestown could be included in the itinerary of a projected visit to the U.S.A. Time was found to take the children to the pantomime. "Is he a real cat?" asked Princess Anne, when introduced to Dick Whittington's cat, to be reassured "He is a real pantomime cat." But the radio-telephone and airmailed sound tape were links with Prince Philip, though rather uncertain ones when he was as far away as Graham Land and Tristan da Cunha.

"The Lord watch between me and thee when we are absent from one another," he had said in a broadcast, knowing that his words would reach the Queen with special significance. In another mood, Prince Philip reported the "appalling smell" of the penguin rookeries of Antarctica. But there was an appalling smell closer to home in the ugly rumours that went into circulation literally behind his back, early in 1957. Every visit that Prince Philip had paid to his relatives in Germany, every minor absence from home, was now distilled into murmurs of evil gossip. On the preceding Christmas Day the Queen had said, "It is sad for us to be separated and of course we look forward to the moment when we shall again be together," and with this was coupled a special wish to "every man or woman whose destiny it is to walk through life alone." Members of the Household were not unaware of the more sophisticated table talk in the metropolis, inventing a completely mythical "rift" between herself and her husband.

In Prince Philip's absence, Princess Marie-Louise, granddaughter of Queen Victoria, died in December, 1956, when the memoirs which Queen Elizabeth had urged her to write were still fresh in every bookshop. In January, 1957, Queen Mary's brother, the Earl of Athlone, followed her to the grave, and for the second time within a few weeks the Queen attended a funeral at St. George's Chapel, Windsor. In this mournful atmosphere, with the ache of the annoying rumours of her own deeper unhappiness still upon her, the Queen completed the fifth year of her reign.

Within ten days of the anniversary of her accession, however, Her Majesty flew in a Viscount airliner to join Prince Philip in Portugal. Here they were to undertake a four-day State Visit. But President Lopes had agreed to reverse the protocol so that a private visit would precede the State functions, permitting the royal couple to spend a happy weekend aboard the *Britannia*. The Queen's Viscount touched down at Montijo airport precisely as the Duke's car drove on to the airfield. And a moment later she rode away from the airport happily reunited with her husband.

Prince Philip was said to be unenthusiastic about the Portuguese visit, the first official visit paid by a British Sovereign to Portugal since the days of King Edward VII. He detected in the pitch of the cheering that hungry fervour he had often noted in republicans, and the visit was indeed not without nostalgia. The Queen was rowed ashore by eighty red-coated oarsmen in the ancient royal barge of Portugal just as her great-grandfather had been before her. She rode in the antique golden coach, sitting on the refurbished cushions that had once supported Portugal's kings. The Queen was greeted by a dictator, but the people hung out their bed-covers in lieu of banners and waited and waved and cheered as if the spirit of a thousand years of monarchy could not be expunged in five years and forty. The glittering panoply of the cavalry escort, the ceremonial release of ten thousand pigeons to denote the Queen's arrival, the enthusiasm of the crowds, the cries of "Viva! Viva la Rainha!" may have made the visitors wonder whether there was not here a mood deeper than courtesy. Every stopping-place in Portugal renewed the fiesta of welcome. Finally, in Oporto, the pressmen applauded the Queen when she changed from the rather dark interior of her car into the cameramen's open bus in order that the acclaiming crowds could see her clearly. Within minutes the bus was knee-deep in rose petals and confetti, as Portuguese emotion overflowed in a sentimental flirtation with yesterday.

CHAPTER XII

QUEEN IN THE SPACE AGE

O^N OCTOBER 4TH, 1957, Russia launched the first earth satellite, Sputnik I, and so inaugurated a strange and unfathomable new era in human history. The news was still being discussed eagerly when Queen Elizabeth II sat nervously before two television cameras set up in the State Dining Room at Buckingham Palace for her first television rehearsals. The space age had begun and the thirty-one-year-old Queen, determined to conquer a new medium, had agreed to broadcast to her Canadian peoples by television from Ottawa on October 13th.

It was twenty-five years since her grandfather made the first Christmas radio broadcast and after the criticism of her 1956 Christmas sound broadcast Her Majesty recognized that she must progress to vision. Television was indeed a medium her husband had already conquered, first in short talks and then in longer programmes. In July the B.B.C. made a film to demonstrate the various techniques available to her: to chat impromptu or frankly read a speech, to read while glancing at the camera occasionally or to look directly at the camera all the time, watching the words of her script flashed before the lens by teleprompter. The Queen studied this instructive film at Balmoral and, guided by Prince Philip's experience, chose the teleprompter method.

It was the responsibility of the B.B.C. team at the Palace to rehearse the Queen and make a telerecording to guide Mr. Michael Hand-Smith, the C.B.C. producer in Canada. The Queen did a run-through and then a "take." Her face was taut, her normally low and pleasant voice strained and high in pitch through nervousness. The producer pointed out these beginner's mistakes and she tried another run-through, but next day the Queen and her husband saw and heard both the telerecordings and found them so disastrous that the Queen decided, on the Duke's suggestion, to scrap them and do the whole thing again.

Meanwhile, Her Majesty had to have an inoculation for Asian flu, then rife in America, and to rehearse the script of a speech to the United Nations. Time was needed for her hairdresser and for last-minute wardrobe fittings. The following day, a Thursday, she had just returned from the memorial service to King Haakon of Norway when two more telerecordings were made. On Friday the results were viewed in the Palace billiard-room, and, still short of the desired effect, a telerecording "for guidance only" was flown to Canada.

The royal couple themselves left London airport at 7 A.M. Saturday, arriving in Ottawa that afternoon. That same evening the Queen achieved the extraordinary feat of shaking hands with five hundred people in under an hour at a Press reception. Next day she laid a wreath at the cenotaph and attended Divine Service at Christ Church

Cathedral. But that afternoon she was still miserable with nervousness as she undertook her television rehearsals and faced the first hurdle of the tour, the broadcast.

The Queen kicked off her shoes as she sat at the desk for the run-through, but the producer noticed the "expression of congealed terror" in her eyes as the broadcast was about to begin. Prince Philip had, however, a card of his own to play. "Tell the Queen to remember the wailing and gnashing of teeth," he directed. The phrase obviously had some special meaning. The mystified director did as he was bid. The Queen flashed a smile of instant amusement and next moment, visibly eased, she was on the air.

"When my husband and I were leaving Canada last time, in the teeth of a gale, as you may remember, we heard kindly people at Portugal Cove singing, 'Will ye no come back again?' Now, after six years, I want you to know how happy I am to be in Canada, once again, particularly at Thanksgiving. . . ."

The broadcast was a long one, in both English and French. "There are long periods when life seems a small dull round, a petty business with no point, and then suddenly we are caught up in some great event . . ." the Queen drew to her conclusion. "I hope that tomorrow will be such an occasion."

This first broadcast was proclaimed a triumph. Relaxed and free, the Queen probably found no ordeal in the great event she had in mind, the opening of the Canadian Parliament, when she wore her Coronation gown and read the Speech from the Throne under strong lights that brought the temperature to ninety-three degrees. Could it be claimed that royal speeches were phrased in platitudes? The Queen recalled the words of the first Elizabeth to her last Parliament, *"Though God hath raised me high, yet I count the glory of my Crown that I have reigned with your loves.* Now . . ." Queen Elizabeth II continued fervently, "here in the New World, I say to you that it is my wish that in the years before me, I may so reign in Canada and be so remembered. . . ."

There had been some discussion whether it would be appropriate for the Queen to land in the United States at Patrick Henry Airport, named for the rebel who wanted either liberty from English rule or death. However the Queen landed there by R.C.A.F. plane and tried to make it very clear in four speeches given in the next eight hours that she thought it a wonderful idea to start her visit at the place where the American nation had been born three and a half centuries before. "The settlement in Jamestown was the beginning of a series of overseas settlements made throughout the world by British pioneers. Jamestown grew and became the United States. Those other settlements grew and became nations now united in our Great Commonwealth. . . ."

So said the Queen. The Suez crisis had impaired Anglo-American relations, and in the next four days the Queen restored them. She joked happily about George III. She visited the restored Colonial capital of Williamsburg with appreciation and delight, for was not every brick a reminder of the Anglo-American past? In Williamsburg the whole of the 100-room inn had been prepared for her, and the following night she went to Washington and slept in the White House. "My, you look pretty!" said Mamie Eisenhower in welcoming her.

The rather silent onlookers of 1951 were replaced now

by crowds who cheered with happy noise, as if television had made the Queen a more familiar and friendly figure. At a Press reception she was asked "How do you survive your terrific schedule of appearances?" and she had replied, "I survive by enjoying myself every minute of the day." Now she manifestly enjoyed President Eisenhower's huge bubble-topped car, the novelties of arrangement of the banqueting-table at the White House, a visit to an art gallery where she saw some of her own Blake water-colours on loan, her visit to a football game, and her impromptu exploration of a self-help super-market.

But the most personally memorable day of the tour was doubtless the long-awaited day in New York. Arriving by train from Washington, the Queen sailed across the harbour in an Army ferry so that she might enjoy the famous view of the skyscraper skyline. "Fabulous! Exciting!" she exclaimed, as so many have exclaimed before her. But for the Queen's special greeting guns thundered in salute, bands played, avenues of fire floats flung their feathery columns of water high into the air, and at the Battery a bubble limousine waited for the ticker tape ride up Broadway. "Welcome Liz and Phil!" said every shop window.

Then that afternoon, when the Queen was introduced to the United Nations Assembly, every seat was occupied and people were standing nine deep. Her speech was broadcast to the entire world, filmed and televised.

Later that afternoon, from the top of the Empire State Building the Queen looked down on the city. In the evening she dined with four thousand people at a banquet sponsored by the Pilgrims and the English Speaking Union and afterwards went on to a Commonwealth ball. It was two o'clock in the morning before her plane left Idlewild.

"Strong men have broken covering this royal runaway race," Bob Considine summed up. "There isn't a clear eye left, except Elizabeth's."

In August of 1959 it was a comfort to the Queen to be back in her familiar rooms and to be reassured by her own doctors, Lord Evans, Sir John Weir, and Mr. John Peel. She was just back from a tremendously strenuous Canadian tour. This time she had really met the people. In Canada too she had suspected that she was pregnant. Her highest hopes were confirmed now.

The prospect of a child for the reigning Queen was announced from Buckingham Palace: "The Queen will undertake no further public engagements. Her Majesty deeply regrets the disappointment which her inability to carry out her projected tour in West Africa as arranged this autumn may bring to many of her people in Ghana, Sierra Leone, and the Gambia. Her Majesty also much regrets that she and the Duke of Edinburgh will be unable to visit Shetland and Orkney next week. The Queen, who has been seen by her medical advisers since returning from Canada, is stated by them to be in good health."

The Duke of Edinburgh deputized for the Queen at investitures and, indeed, visited Ghana for a week in November. The expectant mother elected to await her baby chiefly at Sandringham, while the old ladies of the Linen and Woollen Drapers Home at Derby happily knitted and stitched a fifty-six piece white layette. Many humbler gifts, however, inevitably again turned Buckingham Palace into a charitable clearing-house. The Queen was said to have acquired a fondness for honey and the generosity of bee-keepers was instantly alerted. The people

of West Virginia sent a copy of the U.S. Government pub-
lication "Infant Care." The Diplomatic Corps subscribed
for a silver cup for the baby, of the year 1693. The Government of Kenya sent a gift rug of nine lambskins and
a middle-aged lady in South London was discovered to be
retrimming the cradle and nursery hamper used for Prince
Charles and Princess Anne.

When Queen Elizabeth II returned to London on January 18th, the hubbub around the Palace increased. It was
known that Sister Helen Rowe, and Sister Annette Wilson
of King's College Hospital, would attend the Queen, and
the movements of these ladies were dogged with avidity.
The doctors were smuggled in and out of a tradesmen's
entrance while the daily clusters of enthralled bystanders
at the main gates thickened. The salute of guns and ringing of the Westminster Abbey bells for the eighth anniversary of the Queen's accession started a flurry of
rumours. Meanwhile the Queen walked in the Palace
grounds, drove out to tea with friends, dined with the
Mountbattens and quietly went to Harrod's one day to
inspect a new pram.

She was looking into the future, and indeed far into the
future. On February 8th, at a meeting of the Privy Council, she signified her will and pleasure that "while I and
My children shall continue to be styled and known as the
House and Family of Windsor, My descendants other than
descendants enjoying the style, title or attribute of Royal
Highness and the titular dignity of Prince or Princess and
female descendants who marry . . . shall bear the name of
Mountbatten-Windsor." The Queen thus provided that
her husband's name should be preserved among their
great-grandchildren.

The main bedroom of the Belgian Suite had been prepared for the lying-in and the Queen's doctors arrived at
8 A.M. on February 19th. In the wan light of the late afternoon sun, Prince Andrew was born. "It's a boy!" servants
heard Prince Philip calling, and Commander Colville
walked across the Palace courtyard to post the handwritten
bulletin on the railings: "The Queen was safely delivered
of a son at 3.30 P.M. today. Her Majesty and the infant
Prince are both doing well."

It will long be remembered that the birth of Prince
Andrew, a Friday child, heralded a week of strangely
mingled joy and sadness, of bereavement and betrothal.
The following day, one of the Queen's closest friends,
Countess Mountbatten of Burma, died suddenly in North
Borneo, and three days later the Marquess of Carisbrooke,
the last surviving grandson of Queen Victoria, died at
Kensington Palace. Three days more and the Queen
Mother announced Princess Margaret's happy betrothal
to Mr. Antony Armstrong-Jones, "to which the Queen
has gladly given her consent." The Queen herself did not
reappear in public until April 5th.

In the next quiet months the Queen found time to be
her womanly self, to go shopping, to meet her friends and
indulge in purely feminine chatter, even to spend an hour
choosing wallpapers for Sandringham. She and her husband often went to the theatre, unannounced and with
such anonymity that one evening they were ushered into
the wrong seats. At Windsor Castle they began to fulfil
an old dream by supervising the remodelling and furnish-
ing of a set of rooms in the King Edward III Tower in an
entirely new and contemporary manner. Their architects,

Sir Hugh and Lady Casson, were encouraged to commission fabrics and furniture from modern designers and a dozen young artists—including devotees of the extreme abstract school—received the royal patronage. But photographs of these private apartments were not released as the interiors of Clarence House had been ten years earlier. Sharper distinction was being made between the fierce light that beats upon the Throne and the tranquil, informal realm of the Queen's private life.

On April 8th, Prince Andrew Albert Christian Edward was christened in the music-room at Buckingham Palace. His five sponsors—the Duke of Gloucester, Princess Alexandra, Lord Elphinstone, the Earl of Euston, and Mrs. Harold Phillips—were either relatives or the Queen's close private friends. And here again, unexpectedly, there was no film of the royal assembly as there had been for Princess Anne. Not a single commemorative photograph was issued of the occasion, so firmly was the Queen drawing the demarcations of privacy around her third baby. In Prince Andrew's first year no photographs were issued between March and the happy pictures in August taken on the occasion of the Queen Mother's sixtieth birthday. Prince Andrew was in fact sixteen months old when he made his first public appearance. Returning from the 1961 Trooping the Colour on her official birthday, Her Majesty, dressed in her scarlet uniform, walked on to the balcony of Buckingham Palace with the infant Prince in her arms, demonstrating her immense sense of dramatic occasion and pride in her third child.

The Queen could end 1960 with a sense of replenishment and rich fulfilment. The creation of an elegant and private new background of her own at Windsor and Princess Margaret's happy marriage both alike deepened the contentment that sprang from Prince Andrew's birth.

The world-wide travels of Queen Elizabeth II may not strike future generations with the sense of wonder, mission, and swift accomplishment that still affects our own contemporary imagination. Who would have thought that the Queen would enter the tenth year of her reign in the barren landscape of the Khyber Pass, with an embarrassed Pathan tribesman to welcome her with a bouquet of roses and marigolds? The Queen herself did not foresee that she would cut a cake for Prince Andrew's first birthday surrounded by sari-clad women in the sultry February atmosphere of Madras. Who could have imagined during the bitter birth-pangs of India in 1947 that within a brief fourteen years thousands of Union Jacks would flower in Delhi and find India's millions demonstrating their affection and friendship for the embodiment of the Raj? Who would have known that within five years of the dark bloodshed in Cyprus the Queen would meet Archbishop Makarios as President of the Republic of Cyprus and restore "the final seal of friendship"?

It was said that the 1961 visit to Ghana, Sierra Leone, and the Gambia indicated the shape of future royal journeys, that henceforth the strenuous protracted tour belonged to the past. The Queen has acquired a wider experience of the physical face of the globe than any other woman on earth. And yet still she has not seen Antarctica or the Arctic. South-East Asia has not been visited nor South America. State Visits are still to be returned to Germany and to Ethiopia. The countries of the Iron Curtain seem secluded, but who can prejudge the unsuspected possibilities of the nascent future? The year 1962 was planned to be "a restful year," but who can tell what hopes may be fulfilled, what great events may gleam among the dross of unremitting effort?

The Queen completes the first decade of her sovereignty and this is only a threshold, under Providence. We may glance reminiscently at Queen Victoria and judge that ten years on the throne was only the forenoon of her long reign. The decades ahead will bring change and events that none can foresee, and yet we know that the Queen will be steadfast, a part of world history, each day mindful of her peoples, each day at her assiduous and dedicated task, perhaps no day of all our era without the shaping of her signature,

ELIZABETH R.

(WHOM GOD PRESERVE)

Date Due

JUN 2 1969		
SEP 22 1976		
NOV 7 1970		
JY 0 8 '70